Lowell Green

[signature: Lowell Green]

How the granola-crunching, tree-hugging thug huggers are wrecking our country!

Creative Bound International Inc.
www.creativebound.com

ISBN 978-1-894439-30-5
Printed and bound in Canada

Pre-press and production Creative Bound International Inc.

Library and Archives Canada Cataloguing in Publication Data

Green, Lowell, 1936-
     How the granola-crunching, tree-hugging thug huggers are wrecking our country / Lowell Green.

Includes bibliographical references.
ISBN-13: 978-1-894439-30-5
ISBN-10: 1-894439-30-9

     1. Canada—Social conditions—21st century. 2. Canada—Politics and government—2006-. I. Title.

FC640.G74 2006   971.07   C2006-905833-4

To the
"CFRA Nation"
which has never
let me down.

Contents

ONE

Why?

Multiculturalism, bilingualism, biculturalism, medicare, the Charter of Rights and Freedoms, peacekeeping, gay marriage, mass immigration, our open-arms refugee policy, Kyoto, the Young Offenders Act, needle exchange programs…all are, or have been, defining social policies of Canadian life. All appear to have evolved in isolation, independent of each other, sometimes at different times in our history. And yet close examination reveals a rather startling fact: They all spring from the same mindset, the same view of the world and of Canada. To put it in perhaps more understandable terms, the NDP strongly supports every single one of the policies that I have listed.

How did this happen? How could it be that virtually every major social policy in this country conforms to the agenda of a socialist political party supported by less than 20 percent of the popular vote?

In many instances these policies just showed up on our doorsteps one day with no kind of parliamentary or national debate. We all awoke one morning to discover that we were now a multicultural nation. That was just shortly after we were all informed in no uncertain terms that we were a bicultural nation. Our fighting military heritage was replaced by peace-keeping without anyone asking us. Kyoto was signed by the Chrétien government with most Canadians entirely unaware of the implications while large numbers of our leading scientists believe human-induced global warming is a hoax.

Who are the people who made these decisions for us? How were they able to convince the bulk of Canadians that their vision of Canada is the one that should prevail? How did so many of us come to confuse socialist ideology with wisdom even when it leads to disaster?

Most importantly, what can we do to start reversing some of the engines propelling us toward a dangerous cliff? A cliff over which many other socialist nations have already tumbled.

First we must identify the enemy and the weapons they use!

TWO

The Age of Wisdom

My wife, who knows such things, says that according to the famed psychoanalyst Erik Erikson, I have now entered the age of wisdom. Which delights me since I was beginning to believe my increasing inability to deal with political correctness, bafflegab, and buffalo chips is due entirely to creaky knees and a declining golf game!

I'm not making any claims that my brain power is superior, or even that it matches that of the great minds which have run and continue to run things around here. No doubt many of them have spent far more time than I at what my grandfather used to call "book learning," but according to Erikson that's not necessarily wisdom. Wisdom, he says, is achieved in the final stage of human life, "the integrity phase," and can best be described as the ability to utilize knowledge, experience, and common sense coupled with insight that is hopefully acquired after many years of keen observation.

I have certainly had many years of observation, some at least reasonably keen!

After my wife informed me of this wisdom thing, I got to

thinking that there is probably no one in this country who has discussed, debated, and downright argued with as many people about as many important issues as I. Similarly, I doubt very much if there is anyone in the country who has paid as close attention to daily events and their ramifications for as long as I. Thus it is that I am not sure whether it is the wisdom of my advancing years or the practical knowledge acquired from spending almost 50 of them at a microphone talking to thousands of people that has convinced me we're doing just about everything we can to screw up what used to be a perfectly good country.

Just to give you an idea of how long I've been at this talk-show business, and how much the nation's mores have changed, when I started "The Greenline" in Ottawa in 1966 I could not use the word "pregnant" on air. Any reference to an impending birth had to be extremely circumspect—"in the family way" was the usually preferred description. "Blessed event" also received the censors' seal of approval. I came close to spending a few nights in jail when in 1967 I allowed someone on the show to talk about birth control. Until Trudeau came along and told us government had no business in the bedrooms of the nation, it was illegal, and a very serious offence, to discuss any form of birth control in public.

We've come a long way, baby! Not all of it necessarily in the right direction!

Call it wisdom, call it common sense, call it what you like, but one of the things I see that has really begun to screw up the country is our amazing inability to learn from past mistakes.

There is an element in this country, for the most part on what I call the hard Left of the political spectrum, which simply cannot bring itself to admit that when a policy continually fails or even exacerbates the problem, it is time to change direction, try something new, learn from failure. In many instances, some of these people are so blinded by ideology that they do not recognize failure, or even disaster as such.

Later in this book, I will give you example after example of where policies which have clearly failed are continued for no other reason than those who promoted those policies have convinced themselves and much of the rest of the country that failure is really success! That disaster is really triumph! And in the process, many unwary Canadians have been persuaded to ignore the way the world really works in favour of a rose-coloured vision of how they would like it to work.

Much of our social policy as it applies to family values, crime, education, immigration, the environment, multiculturalism, health care, even bilingualism, is based not on reality but on a politically correct utopian dream.

If Erikson is right, if I have truly entered the age of wisdom and have a duty to try and share some of it, then I must have passed through its portals on a cold and rainy night in 1993 in Toronto when Helen called...

THREE

The Call

It's been more than 12 years but the call still gives me night-mares! Helen is her name. She is probably still in shock. Her voice is almost too calm. Her words chilling. "My father died right out in front of your building last night," she says. "They walked right over top of him. They were so anxious to get on the damn streetcar they stepped right over him. They could tell he wasn't some falling-down drunk. He was dressed in a three-piece suit, for heaven's sake. He was a businessman having a heart attack during rush hour on St. Clair Avenue in down-town Toronto and no one could spare him a minute." She hes-itates for a moment, her voice beginning to break. "The last thing he must have seen was people's legs walking right over him. Is our civilization starting to crumble?" She begins to cry. "What they did to my father. Was that civilized?"

I am dumbfounded. All my years of hosting radio talk shows has not prepared me for this.

The call comes near the end of my evening show on Toronto's CFRB, at that time the most listened to radio station in Canada. The question I posed was whether the Canadian civilization as we knew it was beginning to deteriorate. Most callers seemed to think it was and related stories that proved, to them at least, that while the country may not be going to hell in a handcart, we are faced with very serious decay—moral and otherwise.

The first call of the evening sets the tone. It's from a woman who only a couple of weeks previously had smashed her car into a pole on Avenue Road. "I'm lying there behind the wheel," she says, "my head feels like someone's taken a sledge hammer to it, I'm bleeding like a stuck pig when this guy comes rushing over, rips open the car door, grabs my purse, which has fallen onto the floor, and runs off. For all he knew I was dying. He couldn't have cared less. I couldn't believe it. We're not living in a civilized society anymore. It's a bloody jungle!"

As I recall, there were a few calls a bit more uplifting than that, a couple of the stories were actually kind of funny, but for the better part of three hours it was mostly a chapter from the sorry side of life in the big city today.

A mugging with dozens of people standing around unwilling to help. A father in a fit of road rage giving the finger and screaming some unpleasantness at another driver, undeterred by the two kids in his back seat. Teen punks cursing and swearing in the back of a bus; that sort of thing. None of it supporting the thesis that we are building a better society in this country.

And then finally the call from Helen. Only one young woman had stayed at the streetcar stop with her dying father. "I asked several people to dial 911," she told Helen, "I'm not sure if anyone even did that. Most people wouldn't even look down as they stepped over him to get their ride home." By the time an ambulance arrived it was too late. Sad, sad, sad.

There was a time when that kind of callous disregard for human life would have been shocking. Not today. Nothing in our society today seems to shock us anymore. Being shocked at human behaviour in Canada today seems kind of old-fashioned, quaint even.

'What's happening to us?" ask several callers. "Where are we headed? How did we let this happen?"

As usually occurs in discussions of this nature, responses to those questions range from the ridiculous to the sublime but almost everyone seems to agree on one thing: Canadian civilization is in a serious state of decline. And after some urging from me, all agree that there *is* such a thing as a Canadian civilization. Not as powerful, not as influential as the American civilization, but nonetheless distinct. Surely most of us agree that we are different here in Canada. We are a people quite distinct from any other. We are different from the European civilizations from which most of us sprang and different as well from the American. Most callers agree that one thing we share with the American civilization is that we find ourselves facing very serious decay, moral and otherwise. The Canadian civilization, like the American, is in decline. When I suggest that this decline is occurring while European and some Asian civilizations are in the ascendancy, I meet with serious opposition. The consensus that night on my CFRB show was that Western civilizations, right across the board, are in decline.

One of the more intelligent callers suggests the decline—the decay—is not political—"it is not economic either," he says. "Those are only the symptoms. It has to do with the question of our entire way of life—our civilization is unravelling around us."

It's awfully hard not to agree. Everywhere you look you see evidence of it. You don't have to go back to a Toronto talk show more than a decade ago to see it and hear it. Even as I am writing this book, a caller to my show on CFRA in Ottawa steadfastly maintains that an extra ten dollars a month on his pension is just as important as anyone's life. We are discussing a threatened strike by some 120,000 CUPE workers that, among other things, would take some ambulances and paramedics off the road. I suggest that there has to be a better way. "Surely," I tell the caller, "you wouldn't be prepared to risk your mother's life for an additional ten dollars a month on your pension!" "I certainly would," he asserts. "They are of equal value." He later informs me that his mother is dead so the question isn't relevant. "Is an extra ten dollars a month on a pension worth risking anyone's life?" I ask. "Absolutely," he replies once again. "They are of equal value." When he refuses to rethink his statement, I tell him he is a disgusting human being, and boot his sorry butt off the air but I have no doubt whatsoever that his views are widely held.

It's not that long ago that striking Montreal firemen cut hoses when supervisory staff tried to quell a major blaze that threatened many lives!

In Toronto, a sad little six-year-old boy slowly dies of hunger, thirst and dreadful neglect. Even as he loses more and more weight, can barely talk or walk, professional childcare workers don't spot anything wrong. Or at least they say they don't! Boarders living in the house see the slow murder but don't do anything for fear of being evicted. It's not their problem!

And let's have a look at crime in general. If ever there was an example of how we continue to adhere to terribly failed policies, surely it is in the field of crime and punishment. Despite all the evidence (and there is plenty of it) that so-called "soft justice" does not work, we continue to pretend that it does.

We are being told that the overall crime rate is down slightly in the past few years, but that is a gross misrepresentation of the facts. Don't take my word for it, check out an editorial that appeared in the *Ottawa Sun* on April 24, 2006, a few days after Stephen Harper introduced his get-tough-on-crime package to the Commons. In it, the *Sun* says: "Violent crime in Canada today is 35 percent higher than it was just 20 years ago." You read that right. It's from last year's Statistics Canada report on the crime rate.

But how is this possible, you're asking? Hasn't the "hug-a-thug" crowd constantly told us that crime is going down and thus there is no need to toughen our laws?

Well, what liberal politicians, academics and pundits have been doing is quoting the statistics very selectively. It's true that after peaking in 1991, violent crime has been dropping slowly. Today it's down about 10 percent from a decade ago. But those who want to coddle criminals don't tell you that this very slight decline has in no way matched the explosion in violent crime that started in the 1960s and continued for 30 years. The real story is that violent crime today is at levels that would have been considered appallingly high only two decades ago.

If, in fact, crime in Canada has declined slightly in the past few years, it surely has as much to do with our citizens locking themselves into little fortresses at night as it does any improvement in the moral climate. Playgrounds go empty because parents won't let their children walk down the block unescorted. In some of our buildings, seniors cower in their tiny apartments most of the day, afraid to even venture into the hallways where very often punks, prostitutes, and pimps have taken over. I will never forget one woman's anguished call to my show. "I went to get on the elevator in my building last night," she said, "two people were having sex and asked me if I wanted to join in!" There are some, I suppose, who might think that kind of thing is funny, unless of course the victim happened to be their mother trying to live out the last few years of her life in peace and security.

One thing we are all only too familiar with is the frightening escalation of juvenile crime, especially violent juvenile crime that is up about 126 percent since 1986 (Statistics Canada Report on Crime 2005).

But our decaying civilization cannot be measured in crime figures alone; that is only one indicator. Ancient Rome didn't have a whole lot of crime, mainly because you'd get fed to the lions for stealing a loaf of bread or crucified for challenging religious beliefs. Rome's decay went much deeper than that. It had to do with the moral fibre of its people—once the bravest, most daring, most civilized in the world, or certainly since the ancient Greeks.

The story of the Romans and the Greeks, who created marvellous civilizations and then allowed them to rot away from within, is a story which has been repeated throughout history. There have been a great number of Neros fiddling away while our cities and our civilizations burn.

• • •

One measure of the temper of our moral decay is the approximately 40,000 federal public servants, living in Quebec, who just prior to the 1995 Quebec Referendum signed a deal with Jacques Parizeau assuring them of equal-paying jobs in the new Kingdom of Quebec. Most of the 40,000 saw nothing wrong with workers accepting pay from Canadian taxpayers while signing a deal with the enemy!

More recently of course, the same Union recommended that its members support several separatist candidates in the Outaouais. Gatineau did just that during the January 2006 election, electing a separatist. Thousands of federal public servants voted for a party that wants to break Canada apart, while accepting cheques every week from Canadian taxpayers.

Not very good value for the billions of dollars we have spent trying to buy the loyalty of Quebec francophones!

The decay can also be measured by the fact that in the fall of 2003, the education of some 16,000 of our children was threatened by an Ottawa teachers' work-to-rule and school board lockout, even as three million dollars was paid out to teachers for unused sick leave. Obviously both the school board and the teachers believe that paying millions of dollars in unused sick leave to retiring teachers takes precedence over educating our children.

Today, at a time when our education system slips further and further behind that of most European and Asian nations, it is widely reported that we in Ontario owe more than one billion dollars in unused sick leave pay to retiring teachers! Strikes affecting the education of tens of thousands of school children across Canada are commonplace because we as a nation cannot agree that education is a basic right and that methods of settlement which do not use children as pawns must be adopted.

A recent *US News Today* story reported that fully 76 percent of American children graduating from high school cannot read or write at a level European Union nations now deem appropriate for entry into university. We don't have comparable figures in Canada since we don't have universal testing, but most people who know anything about it will admit we are only marginally ahead of the Americans, if at all.

Here's another scary thought: A recent test indicated that the average Canadian high school graduate was at least two years behind students of the same age in India. In science we are so far behind most Asian countries we are hardly in the race.

You don't need nationwide tests to prove any of this. Just check around the neighbourhood. We have a friend whose ten-year-old daughter has just been tested and found to have reading and math comprehension at the grade-two level. She's in grade five!

In my opinion, failure to make the education of children the highest priority is an indication of a civilization in decline. Nothing should take precedence over education, especially in today's global economy. Common sense dictates that if our children cannot compete in the classroom it is only a matter of time until the country itself cannot compete with better educated populations. Sadly, in Canada today the education of our children seems to take a back seat to union contracts, tenure, province-wide negotiations, school board amalgamations, pension plans, prep time, PD days, and sick leave.

Listen, if this was a great civilization and not one in decline, here is what we would do: We would tell our schools, "You must educate at least 76 percent of the students who come to you to an accepted international level or we will find someone else who can." If 76 percent of high school graduates can't read or write at an international level, close the school down and start all over again. Get new administrators, new teachers, find someone who can do the job and if the next bunch we hire can't do it properly fire them and get someone who can. They can do the job in India. They can do the job in Korea, in France, in Germany—then, by damn, we'll do it here in Canada.

But would we ever do anything even close to that here? Not on your life. The malaise is so deep that even robbing our children of a proper education has not as yet motivated us to take action we all know should be taken—must be taken—if we are to compete globally.

Much of the decline is crazily enough the result of good intentions. We have always fancied ourselves in Canada as a kinder, gentler people. The 16-year-old doesn't get along with his old man; no problem, get on the government nipple. The taxpayers will look after you. It's the merciful thing to do, goes the mythology, at least the mythology of the Left, the ones I often only half jokingly describe as the granola-crunching, tree-hugging thug huggers.

The 14-year-old single mother; no problem, no shame, no chasing the father, just come on board the welfare train; we'll look after you and, by the way, if you want some more children, that's just fine and dandy too. The more you have the more we'll pay you and as an extra bonus we'll absolve you of all blame and responsibility; we'll pretend it's all society's fault.

Whatever you do, don't even think about raising the issue of morality. That's an outdated judgmental word. The state owes you anything you want.

And how about the 26-year-old assembly line worker who gets laid off? What do we say to him? Hey man, no way you should drive a cab or flip burgers. That's beneath you, man. You're entitled to the same wages and benefits you were getting before. Take a lower-paying job? Are you nuts? That's just the capitalist swine trying to take advantage of you. Besides which, if you don't have a job it's the government's fault.

All done, at least originally, with the best of intentions. The Left, the political and intellectual elites, have most of us convinced this is the way to go. Many of us honestly believe we can measure a nation's compassion by the number of people we have on welfare.

When Mike Harris came along and cut welfare payments by about 20 percent, within a year the welfare rolls in Ontario dropped by more than 200,000 people. Almost all got jobs, something most logical people would think was a wonderful thing. Logic, unfortunately, is pretty much a stranger to large numbers of Canadians, which explains their response. Many screamed bloody murder! Terrible, discrimination, cruel, the cuts are killing people, it's outrageous was the mantra of many of my callers with echoes across the country. Some of the NDP's leading lights went so far as to predict widespread rioting. "People will be dying in the streets," I even had callers proclaiming.

Think of it. Mike Harris in his first four years as Premier saw an increase of some 700,000 jobs in Ontario. The welfare rolls were cut in half, thousands of people who had never worked a day in their lives before went out and got a job, but to this day the majority of Ontarians will tell you this was a very bad thing!

All of this after just one generation of socialism. Imagine what it will be like when our grandchildren begin running things! Unless, of course, we straighten them out.

FOUR

It's Not My Fault!

At Kingston is a penitentiary that at one time housed both Karla and Paul. Paul, as you know, is still there. Karla—well that's another story thanks to the "Buffalo Bob" Rae Government that signed off on her sweetheart deal. Or, as some would say, the deal with the devil! At the rear of that penitentiary are a number of sheds—almost truck-like in appearance. The prisoners, as you can imagine, call them something not exactly politically correct. Last word, trucks. First word rhymes with truck. You get the picture! Officially they are known as conjugal visitation modules. Not a bad idea actually. Behave yourself in jail and you'll get a couple of hours' privacy with your wife, or whomever.

But here again the kinder, gentler people, the granola-crunching thug huggers can't get it right. The trucks may have to be discontinued. Why? Because misguided souls in charge won't allow body searches of the visitors. It would contravene their privacy rights. As a result, this has become the main conduit of smuggled drugs into the prison. Even those inmates who want no part of smuggling have no choice. Either sneak the stuff into the cells or get a lead pipe in a place that can cause major damage! In our effort not to contravene human rights we totally abandon logic and, as often happens, trample on human rights.

That's the great problem with the socialist approach. In their efforts to create this great egalitarian, utopian society where everyone takes public transit, where we all recycle everything and the government takes care of us from birth to death, they fail to take into account a basic fact of life: We are not all equal, never have been, and never will be. It just isn't human nature. And, oh yes, something else very important. We are not all nice people!

Yes, we should do everything in our power to provide equal opportunity for everyone, but that doesn't mean we will all end up equal.

Our society should act as a launching pad. Do everything we can to make sure we have an equal amount of rocket fuel for the launch, but after that it's up to the individual. By no means is everyone going to make it to the moon. Heck, some won't even make it much past the tops of the trees!

Those who truly cannot help themselves require our assistance, of course. One problem is we're so busy with handouts to people who should be looking after themselves there's almost nothing left over for those truly in need.

Look around, please. See who is getting the government's money. What you will find, for the most part, is that the money goes to special-interest groups, those who can scream, threaten (the unions), and beg the loudest, or have the best lobbyists in Ottawa. And, of course, a fair chunk of our money goes to a few favoured businesses. The Canadian Taxpayers Federation says that while some three billion dollars has been loaned out to a few major corporations such as Honeywell and Bombardier in the last ten years, less than five percent of our money has been returned to us!

One of the last House of Commons speeches delivered by Charles Penson, Conservative member from Peace River, Alberta, before his retirement from Parliament in 2005 blasted the government for "handing out billions of dollars in so-called loans to various profitable companies." Declared Penson, "Those aren't loans. Those are outright grants. At least call them what they really are. Tell the truth." [Source: Hansard, the official verbatim report of the debates in the House.]

Think you could get a deal like that from your bank? Ha!

Now look around and see who really needs our help, and how much they get. In Ontario, disabled people are expected to live on a pension of $940 a month. Many seniors who have worked all their lives to help build this country are in desperate straits. The last time I checked, the allotment of baths in government nursing homes had been reduced to two a week. There's just no money left for people who honestly need and deserve our help!

On the other hand we are telling those who could and should be looking out for themselves, especially our young people, that they have no means of self-determination. That they are virtually powerless against the terrible forces of capitalism.

Perhaps unwittingly, our new Governor General fell into the trap of downplaying individual responsibility when she addressed the Ontario Legislature on February 20, 2006:

> While our society must fight crime, it must also get at the roots of crime. Too many Canadians, here in Toronto, in Northern Ontario and across the country are relegated to the margins and left to fend for themselves."

She then continued:

As I stated in my installation address, nothing in today's society is more disgrace-ful than the marginalization of some young people who are driven to isolation and despair. We must not tolerate such disparities.

She talks about Canada having the financial resources to address these problems, but unfortunately ignored any sugges-tion that young people, or old, have a responsibility to make every attempt to rise above circumstance. Also lacking, in my opinion, was a reminder to all that, no matter what marginal-ization may or may not have occurred, there is never any excuse for committing criminal acts.

Her message, it seems to me, is one we hear only too fre-quently in this country—that the young people shooting each other in Toronto, the ones mugging, stealing, swarming, and raping aren't really responsible for their own actions. It's soci-ety's fault, a message that is pounded into our heads from birth these days in this country.

Many members of our society, and not just the youth in Toronto, are of the firm belief that they are entitled to the good life, and if they do not obtain it, it's everyone else's fault. Further-more, it's their "right" to go out and get their piece of the pie even if it belongs to someone else. If you listened closely to the testimony at the Gomery inquiry, you heard variations of that theme repeatedly. And what was it that David Dingwall had to say about being "entitled to his entitlements?"

Small wonder, I suppose, that there are some who honestly believe that if someone happens to have a jacket they want or looks at them the wrong way, they deserve to get shot. Besides which, the shooters were driven to it. Haven't you been listen-ing to all those smart people out there claiming that young people are getting the shaft these days, not being treated fairly? You can almost hear the thugs saying, "Right on. The man's got it right. It ain't our fault we shooting people. We marginalized! We despairin'! That's why we shootin'!"

The thugs are by no means alone in holding society responsible for their failed aspirations. With some notable exceptions, most Canadians still believe the government should create highly paid, secure-for-life jobs and then find them for us. Even more serious than that, it has created a huge subculture that believes it has no responsibility for itself.

Not only no responsibility for ourselves, for goodness' sake. How about no responsibility to raise our own children? Right across Ontario, and for all I know in other provinces as well, we are feeding thousands of children breakfast in our schools. In some cases, we're even providing high school students with free breakfasts in our schools! What's next? Free drugs? (Actually, in some cities we do provide free drugs, free needles and condoms too). All of this is done, as usual, with the best of intentions.

We are told that many of these young people would go hungry otherwise, but the fact is, by feeding students at school we are absolving their parents of that responsibility. And let me tell you something. If, in fact, these kids really are so poor that they come to school starving, we had better have a much closer look at what is going on in the home. No matter what the family income, there is absolutely no excuse for sending a child off to school with an empty stomach. With all the social programs, social workers, food banks, and church organizations, the only reason a child doesn't get breakfast in this country is because his or her parents just can't be bothered. And, of course, if the school is going to feed your child for you, as far as some parents are concerned, "hey, why should I bother?"

All we are doing with programs such as this is making it easier for parents and their children to abdicate their responsibility. Lovely message we are sending!

Some communities take a much more responsible position. In Laval, Quebec, for example, a committee of parents has been established to work in concert with the teachers. If a teacher in Laval spots a child they don't believe is being fed properly, they alert the committee. Someone on the committee then phones the parents to ask if there is a problem. Nine times out of ten the parents didn't even realize the kid was hiking off to school without breakfast and the problem is solved immediately. If it is discovered that there is a real problem, someone on the committee puts the parent in touch with an organization that can help. All very quietly so as not to embarrass, but all intended to illustrate to both parent and child that they have personal responsibilities which at the very least require them to put some food in empty stomachs!

Which approach do you think is the best? Surely the answer is obvious. Why then do we insist in most of the rest of the country on doing something that at best is applying a temporary bandage to what could very well be a life-threatening hemorrhage? Is it because we are just too afraid to tackle the real problem? That we ourselves have fallen victim to the concept that personal responsibility is an outmoded concept?

Maybe this is why we now have people suing McDonald's if they spill hot coffee on themselves. Today even the law agrees that if you get drunk at your friendly neighbourhood bar, sneak away and crash your car, it's the poor beggar who served you the beer who runs the risk of being held responsible.

Could this be why those commuters in Toronto stepped over a dying man rather than stopping or calling for help? Do you suppose they truly believed it just wasn't their responsibility?

One of my father's most delightful stories was about growing up in a village of chimney watchers. On cold mornings everyone checked his or her neighbour's chimney to make sure smoke was rising. No smoke meant possible trouble.

It has truly been a long, long trail a winding from a time when we watched each other's chimneys. And of this I am certain: All the state-run, unionized daycare programs, all the school breakfast programs, all the social programs, all the free needles and crack pipes in the world aren't going to convince many amongst us to start looking out for each other's chimneys, or anything else except, of course, ourselves.

FIVE

The Thug Huggers

"Holy, old mouldy, look at that!" My brother Paul, at the time a sergeant with the Brantford Police Service, doesn't talk to himself all that often, but then again he doesn't see a guy stealing a television set in broad daylight that often either. Paul has just pulled his cruiser around a corner in one of Brantford's ritzier neighbourhoods when what should appear before his amazed eyes but a guy balancing a brand new TV on his shoulder trying to look casual as he strolls across a well-manicured front lawn.

There's been a rash of break-ins in the district so there's no chance this guy is just out for a bit of afternoon exercise. Besides which, Paul has arrested our TV-carting friend a couple of times previously and knows him very well. Not a person you would want to invite in to have a look at your new silverware, believe me!

The television is hurled to the ground and the foot race is on! My brother, having just completed another of his sporadic diet and exercise programs is gaining when the thief jumps into a brand new fire-red Mustang and peels away. Now it's one of your Hollywood favourites—a car chase! Instead of up and down San Francisco's famous hills, this time it's confined to the very ordinary Brantford streets, siren blaring, tires screeching, the Mustang staying well ahead.

It ends suddenly when the Mustang wheels into one of Brantford's seedier low-rent housing complexes. The chasee darts out, romps around the corner and disappears. Several neighbours come running out pointing to a house, which in cop jargon is "well-known to police." "He's in there, he ran in there," they shout. My brother, who once took part in a drug raid on the house, has no doubts whatsoever that the friendly neighbours are correct, but he's got a dilemma. He didn't see our thief-friend go in. Which means Paul can't enter that house, even though he knows full well the crook is inside. He's got to have a warrant.

By this time a couple more cruisers are on the scene. They stand guard while my brother tracks down a friendly judge he knows. It's Saturday afternoon. Finding the judge takes a couple of hours, but it's all for naught. As much as the judge would love to give my brother a warrant so he can go in and arrest this guy, he can't! Why? Because the law says in order to issue a warrant, police must actually see the suspect go into the house. It is simply not good enough to have neighbours indicate the hiding place.

I probably shouldn't tell you this, since these days this kind of thing can get you charged with police brutality or something, but what the heck. You only live once. (Besides which, if they come after Paul with this, he can always claim it wasn't his fault!) Fact is, my brother is not one to let anyone get the best of him, so for months after this little episode, every time one of his officers was having a quiet night, he'd instruct him or her to do a little nighttime check of the house in question. It became a great game. Whip up to the house with the cherry lights whirling, flash the spotlight on the windows, and listen to the toilets flush as thousands of dollars' worth of assorted drugs were sent plunging into the sewers of Brantford! The guy finally took off for parts unknown. "So," says Paul with some satisfaction, "I did my job!"

• • •

You may recall one of the most famous examples of how the thug huggers have tied the hands of police. The RCMP in British Columbia follow a trail of blood from a murdered man's home to a nearby house trailer. The trailer door is covered with bloody handprints. There could be little doubt the murderer is inside. Police yell several times to come out with your hands up, but there is no response. Finally they break the door down and find a man, drunk and covered with blood. They arrest him on the spot and charge him with murder.

Incredibly, the man is let off and police are lectured by the judge for infringing on his rights.

It's called the "hot pursuit" law. What it boils down to is that only in the course of a "hot pursuit," when police actually *see* the suspect going into a house, can they enter without a warrant. Even hearing the suspect inside or, as in the case of my brother, other witnesses seeing the suspect go into the house is not good enough. The only time police can enter a dwelling without a warrant is if it is in the course of "hot pursuit" and police actually see the person enter.

It is only one of a multitude of laws passed in this country at the insistence of left-wing politicians, social activists, lawyers, and in some cases convicted criminals, which have very clearly swung the pendulum of justice far into the accused's corner. More than one caller to my show on CFRA has expressed amazement that police are ever able to make an arrest, let alone get a conviction.

This swing of the justice pendulum in favour of the accused is not confined to Canada. If anything it was much worse in the United States up until recently, when soaring crime rates finally convinced authorities that the lefty thug huggers, once again were dead wrong and that the only things that really deter crime are strict policing and stiff punishment. It's an amazing concept, isn't it? Let would-be criminals know that they will likely get caught and severely punished, and many decide maybe they should take up another line of work.

There is perhaps no more graphic example of how wrong the thug huggers are than what happened in the United States in the 1960s and '70s.

As in Canada, crime rates in the US begin to climb drastically in the 1960s as more and more of us began to buy the Left's insistence that we needed a much softer system of justice. Despite the objections and warnings from most people who knew anything about human nature, we began to provide more and more rights and protections for the accused while at the same time providing fewer rights and protections for the victims. The most graphic example of this happens to be in the United States where in 1966 the Miranda Law was instituted. Thousands of criminals, including hundreds of murders, were set free when courts ruled that police hadn't properly dotted all the i's and crossed the t's.

• • •

The US Supreme Court in the 1960s was the most left-wing and the most activist that country had ever experienced. Just how left-wing is perhaps best illustrated by statements made by Chief Justice David Bazelon in an article he wrote for *Atlantic Monthly* magazine in July 1960. In the article, entitled "The Imperative to Punish," he stated that "the problem with the criminal justice system in the United States is not with the so-called criminal population, but with society whose need to punish is a primitive urge." He went on to suggest that society's need to punish was "highly irrational" and exhibited a "deep childish fear that if punishment was reduced in our prisons the multitude would run amuck." He actually said all of those things and was widely quoted and believed here in Canada, as well.

At one point in the *Atlantic Monthly* article, Judge Bazelon went so far as to ask if it would really be the end of the world if all jails were converted into hospitals or rehabilitation centres. Obviously the Chief Justice of the Supreme Court of the United States could not bring himself to believe that anyone— no matter how horrendous the crime—really needed to be locked up!

He, of course, was only espousing the widely held leftist view that all criminals were really victims themselves, forced into their lifestyle by society's failure to "get to the root cause" of the problem. A view, by the way, expressed by Prime Minister Jean Chrétien speaking in Washington shortly after 9/11.

If any of this sounds like the stuff you hear today from left-wing Liberals, New Democrats, and some segments of the media, say "hey!"

Interestingly enough, back in 1960, both in Canada and the United States, crime was actually decreasing. The murder rate in the US presents the most graphic example of that. On a per capita basis the murder rate in the US in 1960 was about half of what it was in 1930 and, believe it or not, considerably less than it had been in the early 1950s and was dropping.

So what happened when the supporters of "soft justice" the "criminals as victims" crowd got their way and we introduced what they describe as "progressive" methods in the justice system? They told us that a kinder, gentler system of treating the accused and the convicted would greatly reduce the crime rate and make us all much safer. The main reason they introduced the Miranda Law in the States they claimed, was that it would help to protect the lives of police officers. So what happened?

Well, what happened is all hell broke loose!

In Canada we have seen a dramatic increase in crime rates (The *Ottawa Sun* in a piece on April 24, 2006, says 35 percent since 1986) since the introduction of a soft justice system in the early 1960s. In the United States it was an explosion!

Some examples: The US murder rate on a per capita basis more than doubled between 1960 and 1974. The number of police officers killed after the passage of the Miranda Law (1966) tripled in the decade of the 1960s. In the United States, just as in Canada, the new softer laws were especially favourable for juveniles. In Canada, the juvenile crime rate has more than tripled since the passage of the Young Offenders Act. In the United States, the murder rate in the juvenile population more than tripled between 1965 and 1990. (All US crime statistics from the US Department of

Justice, Crime Records; all Canadian statistics from Statistics Canada.)

One of the reasons I am providing the American experience is that while we followed their lead in swinging the pendulum far over to the left-hand corner in favour of the accused and convicted, we are only now under Stephen Harper even talking about following the US lead, admitting the error of our ways, toughening up our laws and reintroducing the concept of punishment.

Because today in the United States the crime rate, especially the violent crime rate, has plunged dramatically. It is especially evident in those cities that have been aggressively fighting crime with more and tougher policing and stiffer sentencing. New York today is hardly recognizable from what it was only 20 years ago.

By now you are probably familiar with former New York Mayor Rudy Giuliani's "broken windows" policy. His theory was that allowing even minor crime, such as broken windows and other forms of vandalism to go unpunished, actually encourages more serious crime.

● ● ●

Mayor Giuliani's first act was to clean up the New York police force by firing those involved in graft and serving notice it would not be tolerated. He then hired hundreds more police officers and empowered them to make arrests for even minor infractions. The common practice of jumping over subway turnstiles was stopped. Interestingly enough, they found that many of those who were doing this were wanted for other offences.

Gangs of youths hanging around street corners were ordered to move along. Kids police thought should be in school were hauled down to a police station and their parents summoned and in some cases fined. Attendance at schools shot up.

The mayor then served notice that he would not allow anyone to live on the streets. You have three choices he warned:

1. Go back to your homes if you have them. If not we'll provide you with decent accommodation;
2. Go into drug or alcohol rehabilitation; or
3. Go to jail.

But *whatever*, we will not allow you to live on the streets. It is unsanitary, unsightly, and unsafe.

The usual suspects on the Left, including most of the Democrats in Congress, screamed bloody murder. There were grave warnings about overflowing jails. Open rebellion on the streets. The usual stuff. We've heard it all before here in Canada.

But guess what? It worked. As soon as police started hauling people off the streets and they realized the mayor meant business, almost all the street people just disappeared. Some did go into rehab and you'll still see a few characters doing a bit of panhandling in New York, but the change is truly miraculous! Even such former hellholes as Harlem are now rapidly becoming middle class and better! And as for the jails...amazing. Just as the mayor and many others predicted, there are fewer people in New York jails today than there were when the crackdown began.

Times Square has even replaced its infamous strip clubs and peep shows with Disney, for heaven's sake. Where once you feared for your life in broad daylight, today you can walk in safety almost anywhere in New York, at night!

As we have seen time and time again, when people realize they will likely get caught and be sentenced to some serious jail time, they decide to take up a career other than crime. (All New York crime figures are quoted in Rudy Giuliani's book *Leadership*, Rudolf Giuliani with Ken Kurson, Miramax Books, Hyperion, New York, NY, 2002.)

Crime has been cut in more than half in many other US cities as a direct response to much tougher law enforcement and longer sentencing.

Despite the evidence, which is plain as the nose on your face, that cracking down on crime is the best way to prevent it, here in Canada the central philosophy of our criminal justice system remains firmly entrenched in that dangerously out-moded concept that providing criminals with more rights and privileges creates a safer society. Any evidence to the contrary is dismissed out of hand. With these terribly naive and misguided people, ideology wins easily any time it is challenged by reality.

Stephen Harper and the Conservatives are going to have a very difficult time changing the mindset of almost all those earning their living from Canada's legal system. Despite all the evidence to the contrary, most of those entrenched in Canada's legal system, from junior law clerks to senior judges, still firmly believe that strict law enforcement and punishment are not deterrents to crime! This is the prevailing belief of the Canadian leftists who, along with such things as conditional sentencing and automatic early parole, have saddled us with the Young Offenders Act. It is just one more example of how we fail to learn from our own mistakes or the successes of others.

As the new Conservative Government announced its plans to toughen up sentencing, Canadian newspapers were filled with editorials, columns, and letters to the editor all claiming that longer jail terms don't deter crime. In the following chapters you can see for yourself what the truth is.

And not just about crime. Anyone who removes the blinders and looks around at other serious problems we are confronted with can clearly see, for example, that despite the tens of millions of dollars we are spending on native reserves, the residents are actually worse off than they were 20 years ago. Ditto the homeless, the street people, and the drug addicts. But we keep doing the same thing, over and over again. More money thrown at the problem, more social workers, more lenient sentencing, more committee meetings, more studies, all resulting in more problems, and more crime.

On the other hand, all around us are perfect examples of how to successfully deal with these issues, but sadly, what actually works just doesn't fit the socialist and very often the anti-American ideology that is rampant in this country and is thus ignored. In many cases what actually works is bitterly attacked.

Opinion is one thing, but it's time to have a close look at some facts which should prove to even the most obtuse skeptic that what's really needed to solve many of our most pressing problems is just a little common sense!

Let's start with crime and the facts involving two fairly major miracles...

SIX

The Miracle of New York

In September 1990, *Time Magazine* ran a cover story head-
lined "The Rotting of the Big Apple." The story described
how New York City had become the crime and welfare capital
of the United States. Violence was out of control. Businesses
were fleeing the city by the thousands, the infrastructure was
crumbling, and the city was bankrupt despite constantly soaring taxes. The *New York Post* carried a headline one day that
filled the entire front page asking desperately "WILL SOME-
BODY PLEASE DO SOMETHING?" It was a legacy of
decades of left-wing liberal policies in a left-wing liberal city
run by left-wing liberal mayors and administrations.

On January 1, 1994, staunch right-wing conservative Rudy
Giuliani, good friend of very right-wing conservative Ronald
Reagan, was sworn in as mayor. He immediately answered the
Post's cry and began to do something.

On January 2, Giuliani summoned Police Commissioner
Bill Bratton to his office. "We've got to show New Yorkers
some hope, some reason to believe that their city can be saved,"
said the mayor. "We can't reduce 2,000 murders a year to none

overnight, we need to tackle something we can accomplish quickly, something visible enough so that people can see the difference right away." He raised the issue of the squeegee people who had been harassing motorists for years.

"The law doesn't allow us to touch them," said Bratton, "unless they become threatening or actually attack someone." "Wait a minute," said the Mayor. "We have jaywalking laws, don't we? Let's see if we can't ticket them for that."

The Police Commissioner was skeptical but returned a few days later excited. "We can do it," he said. "Not only that, we thought there were thousands of these guys, but it turns out there are only 180 in the entire city. We'll put an officer on each one of them and the moment they step off the curb with a bucket we'll ticket them!" And so they did.

Within a few days the squeegee people were gone. As a bonus, police discovered that a number of them were wanted for much more serious crimes and were hauled off to jail. It is now believed that several murders were prevented by this simple act. Rudy and New York had their first victory, small as it was. There were many more!

The following is a brief list of some of the miracles accomplished by eight years of conservative common sense administration in New York City:

- In 1993 there were 1,946 homicides in New York; in 1994, the year Rudy came to power and instituted his broken windows policy, the number declined almost 20 percent to 1,561;
- By 2001, the last year of Rudy's administration, there were 642 murders in New York City, a reduction of 67 percent in eight years;

- Overall crime was reduced 57 percent in the eight years;
- Shootings dropped 75 percent;
- There were almost 1,200 fewer rapes in 2000 compared to 1993;
- Robberies declined from more than 85,000 to just over 36,000;
- Auto theft plummeted from almost 112,000 to fewer than 36,000;
- Burglary dropped from nearly 101,000 to just over 38,000.

One of the most dramatic declines was in the number of violent assaults at the city's Rikers Island Prison—from more than 2,500 violent incidents in 1993 to just 70 in 2001. Until Rudy came along, those who committed violent offences at Rikers, even those who caused serious injury, were hardly ever charged. Rudy insisted that offenders behind bars be charged and sentenced just as they would be in the outside world. The only difference was, the additional sentence was tacked onto the one already being served. As soon as the inmates realized that Rudy meant what he said, the terrible violence slowed dramatically, then virtually stopped.

Amazing, isn't it, how even the behaviour of hardened criminals can be changed with fear? But we shouldn't be surprised. After all, it was fear of our parents that kept most of us on the more or less straight and narrow when we were kids. Today, fearing your parents, or anyone else, is pretty well outlawed, but it's obvious that fear of getting caught and doing some serious jail time is the most effective crime prevention program available.

One of the contributing causes of crime is the knowledge it will not be seriously punished. Evidence abounds in any jurisdiction you care to examine.

Here are two rules you can take to the bank:

- The incidence of crime escalates in direct proportion to the lack of consequences;
- The more crime that goes unpunished, the more crime you will have.

Rudy Giuliani knew it. Today New Yorkers, even the most liberal among them, know it. And well they should because today New York has the lowest crime rate of all major American cities! From the worst, the most dangerous, to the safest. And all it took was eight years of wisdom and common sense!

I won't go into all the other accomplishments of eight years of conservative polices, other than to say it wasn't just the diminution of crime that revolutionized New York. The teacher-pupil ratio was greatly improved. The administration built or renovated more than 73,000 subsidized housing units and acquired more than 2,000 acres of new parkland.

All of this was accomplished while reducing the city payroll by more than 20,000 positions despite greatly increasing the number of police and teachers and substantially lowering taxes!

When Rudy took over New York, the city was bankrupt, pleading for help from other cities. When Rudy moved on, he had a budget surplus of almost $3 billion. The "Big Apple" isn't rotten anymore.

It's much the same story in several other cities. Cleveland, for example, pretty well followed New York's example and is experiencing revitalization akin to that of New York and for the same reasons. On the other hand, cities such as Detroit, where the thug-hugging Left is still firmly in control, things are almost as bad as they ever were. It's not only in Canada where the Left is blinded by ideology!

Here in Canada we're doing things pretty much the way they were in New York before Rudy came along and clamped down. On July 28, 2006, Margaret Wente, writing in the *Globe and Mail*, stated the following:

> In some Toronto neighbourhoods, kids are dodging gunfire in the playground. Stray bullets are flying through the windows of people's homes and landing under their beds. "I don't let my kinds play outside anymore," one mother said. Another said: "My kids were pretty scared. Everyone slept with Mommy last night."

Wente wrote that Toronto City Councillor Michael Thompson remembers growing up as a black kid in a tough neighbourhood but says, "There's a drug culture that's developing in the city of Toronto. And I don't want to support it. I have pictures in my desk of the young boys who've been murdered."

Vancouver has the worst drug problem in North America and, now that Amsterdam is cleaning itself up (according to the *Washington Post*, July 18, 2005), probably the worst drug problem in the Western world.

You will see more panhandlers and street people in downtown Ottawa and Toronto today than you will see in New York.

Fifty-one of us from the Ottawa area were astonished this past spring during a trip to several European cities to discover that the streets of Dublin, Cork, Paris, and London were devoid of panhandlers and, aside from one man sleeping off a drunk in a Dublin doorway, we could see no evidence of the homeless problem that plagues major Canadian cities. In fact, some of the street people we see in Canada may very well be from New York or London. I mean, after all, in many of our cities, Toronto and Ottawa included, we not only provide the street people and druggies with free needles for "shoot 'em ups," but free crack pipe equipment, free condoms, and pretty well free rein to set up housekeeping wherever they choose, including in front of Ottawa and Toronto City Halls, which by the way are far from free!

SEVEN

The California Miracle

It began with two tragedies. In June 1992, beautiful 18-year-old Kimber Reynolds was murdered near her California home by two felons with long prison records. She and her friend Greg Calderson had just finished dessert at a popular Fresno restaurant, The Daily Planet, when two men, riding a stolen motorcycle, grabbed her purse and then shot and killed her. She would have been 19 in four months.

Several months later, October 1993, 12-year-old Polly Klass was kidnapped at her home in Petaluma, California. A country-wide search was launched that ended when her brutalized body was found several months later. Once again the murderer, in this case a man named Richard Allen Davis, was a repeat violent offender. Both cases were widely publicized, and exacerbated by an almost out-of-control crime rate in the state, California residents began to demand, just as in New York, that "somebody do something!" (Strangely, the name of Polly Klass surfaced again recently when police searched Davis's jail cell for any correspondence he might have received from John Mark Karr after Karr claimed he had murdered six-year-old JonBenet Ramsay. No correspondence was found, but Polly's father complained bitterly about the subsequent and unwelcome publicity.)

New York had Rudy Giuliani to clean things up. In California it was Kimber Reynold's father, Mike Reynolds, a wedding photographer, who launched what has become known as the "three strikes you're out law." In fact, Mike tells me, the "three strikes" bill was actually drafted in his backyard only three months after his daughter's violent death.

Despite tremendous opposition from California's powerful left wing, including much of the Democratic Party's political machinery, Proposition 184, as the "three strikes" initiative is called, was placed on the November 1993 referendum ballot and approved with a substantial majority. Proposition 184 substantially lengthened prison sentences for persons who had previously been convicted of a violent or serious crime. Specifically, a person who had been convicted of a prior violent or serious offence and who committed any new felony could receive twice the normal prison sentence for the new crime (the "second strike").

A person who committed two or more prior violent or serious offences and then committed a third new felony would automatically receive 25 years to life in prison (the "third strike").

Proposition 184 was introduced in the California State Legislature in March 1994 and passed into law the following November. The predictions from the "thug-hugging" lobby were many and dire.

Professors from Berkeley University and many of those in the criminal justice system claimed that the state's prisons would be overflowing and the costs would skyrocket. It wasn't fair, they said, it wasn't democratic, but most of all, Californians were assured by the "experts" that it just wouldn't work. Punishment is an archaic concept that is not a deterrent was the mantra of the day.

Well, here we are more than ten years later. What happened in California? Were the thug huggers correct in their claims that punishment is no deterrent? You be the judge.

The following are figures obtained directly from the California Department of Justice, Division of Criminal Information Service. They compare crime statistics over a ten-year period from 1992, some two years prior to the passage of the "three strikes" law until 2002, some eight years after the law was passed. The easiest to understand and the ones that are the most meaningful are those that compare the rate of various crime categories *per 100,000 population:*

- Total crimes dropped from 3,491.5 in 1992 to 1,890.1 in 2002—a reduction of 45.9 percent;
- Total violent crime, down from 1,103.9 in 1992 to 589.2 in 2002, a reduction of 46.6 percent;
- Murder, dropped from 12.5 in 1992 to 8.8 in 2002, a reduction of 45.6 percent;
- Rape, down from 40.7 in 1992 to 28.8 in 2002, a reduction of 29.2 percent;
- Robbery, down from 418.1 in 1992 to 183.6 in 2002, a reduction of 56.1 percent;
- Assault, down from 1,300.9 in 1992 to 632.6 in 2002, a reduction of 45.5 percent;
- Burglary, down from 1,365.2 in 1992 to 672.6 in 2002, a reduction of 50.7 percent;
- Auto theft, down from 1,022.4 in 1992 to 628.3 in 2002, a reduction of 38.5 percent.

An examination of all the statistics reveals that never in history has California seen as dramatic a reduction in every crime category during a comparable time span. Amazingly enough, in 2002, California's overall crime rates had fallen back to the levels seen in 1967. While concrete figures since 2003 are not available, preliminary studies indicate the crime rate continues to follow the same trend—downward.

As for predictions that California would have to build 20 new prisons to accommodate a doubling of the prison population as a result of the "three strikes" law, here are the facts:

California's prison population ten years after the "three strikes" law had increased 25.5 percent, roughly mirroring the increase in the state's population. Furthermore, the prison population stabilized at about 160,000 six years after passage of the law and remained that way for the next four years. Ten years prior to the "three strikes" law, California had to build 19 new prisons. During the ten years after passage of the law, no new prisons had to be built.

According to the California Department of Justice, in the ten years following the "three strikes" law, estimated financial savings to taxpayers of the state was $28.5 billion. Only two states, New York and Massachusetts, have better records of reducing crime over the same period. In both cases it was as a result of more police, more enforcement, tougher laws, and longer sentencing.

Despite the obvious overwhelming success of "three strikes" in California, some residents continue to attack the law, claiming, among other things, it is racist. Proposition 66, an initiative to soften "three strikes," was presented in a referendum in 2004 but voted down. The bleeding hearts, the "experts," and the thug huggers, it seems, just cannot accept the fact that their vision of the world doesn't jibe with reality. The ordinary citizens of California, however, just as in New York, are not blinded by ideology and obviously know a good thing when they see it.

EIGHT

The Squeegee Cult

I have a regular caller to my show on CFRA who's a wonderful conspiracy-theory nutcase! I love talking to this guy, especially on slow days because he's so far out of whack that it puts to shame anything Abbott and Costello ever dreamed up. Among other things, he's convinced that we're all being controlled by a giant "central dark force" through the application of "chem trails."

Most of us are pretty well convinced that the smoke-like trails jet planes often leave behind as they soar through the sky are nothing more than ice crystals, but there's a whole subculture out there that knows better. What's being spread is, in fact, they claim, a diabolical chemical spray that keeps us all under some sort of "mind control." Except, apparently, the people who know about this insidious plot, including my caller. How *they* escape its mind-numbing effects has never been made clear.

So when I got a call from a man who claimed he was organizing local panhandlers into a union, I thought, aha, another nutcase. Maybe I can have some fun. Turns out, this guy was for real. Not only was he forming a panhandlers union, he already had signed up many of them and had recruited some members of Ottawa City Council in joining a fight against the "Safe Streets Act of Ontario." A fight which, incredibly, will likely end up in the Supreme Court of Canada.

The union it turns out is the Industrial Workers of the World, which while it denies being communist, would surely welcome Mr. Marx or Mr. Lenin as a shop foreman. Among other things the IWW (or the Wobblies, as it is sometimes known) promotes is the "working class taking possession of the means of production and abolishing the wage system." Says the IWW constitution: "Instead of the conservative motto a fair day's wage for a fair day's work, we must inscribe on our banner the revolution watchword—abolish the wage system." (If you want to learn more about this group, google "Industrial Workers of the World.")

Imagine, some city councillors in both Toronto and Ottawa wanting to join a court case with a union that once threatened to go to war against capitalists, wants to take over all business in the country and abolish the wage system. This kindred-spirit marriage won't be to lower taxes, nor provide better health care or education, but rather to grant a tiny band of people the right to swipe dirty rags across our car windshields and harass little old ladies heading for church.

Much more than that. If the Safe Streets Act is repealed it means that once again police in Ontario will have no authority to curb aggressive panhandling. Could there be a more graphic example of ideology gone mad?

For years motorists in many of our cities were plagued by louts with dirty rags darting out into traffic at busy intersections, smearing our windshields with a few swipes of unholy, filthy water, then curse, swear, and sometimes pound your car if you didn't fork over a couple of bucks to help finance their next heroin hit. Since this was not only very dangerous but also annoying, it was only natural that the Liberal, and later the NDP Governments of Ontario not only allowed it, but in some ways encouraged the practice. But it really wasn't until some of the squeegee people began to get themselves injured, and in at least one case killed, that they began to attract a cult following.

Despite every indication to the contrary (having elected an NDP government!) some Ontarians had managed to escape the lemmings-over-the-cliff syndrome, dredged up some long-lost common sense and began to object to the intimidation posed by the squeegee people and the risk involved with the practice. The complaints and concerns of sane people, however, were like "throwin' straws against the wind," as my Uncle Yankee Green used to say. In fact, the more complaints and concerns expressed, the more support seemed to build for the squeegee cause. Open-line shows across the province were flooded with calls from people who claimed the squeegee people had no other choice. "They are driven to it," was a common theme (sound familiar?).

I remember one semi-demented woman, almost in tears, insisting on my show that squeegeeing was a "God-given right in Canada." I was reviled and worse for suggesting that darting out into traffic with a brain half-fried with drugs might be a tad bit dangerous. I recall one time insisting that if these people were able-bodied enough to cart around buckets of dirty water and take swipes at windshields, they might be able-bodied enough to get a real job. That revolutionary idea almost caused a riot!

It was the same story in Toronto where newspapers took up the squeegee cry. Columnists maintained, "We must get to the root cause of the problem" (sound familiar?). The squeegee cause grew into a "squeegee cult," threatening even to supplant the "homeless cult."

One of the things Mike Harris promised during the 1995 election campaign was that he would put an end to squeegeeing and aggressive panhandling. And that's exactly what he did shortly after being elected, passing the Safe Streets Act, which banned aggressive panhandling of all kinds, including squeegeeing.

At the time I was receiving numerous complaints that people, especially elderly women, were afraid to attend mass because gangs of panhandlers were harassing parishioners at several local churches. Similar complaints were pouring in from merchants in both Toronto and Ottawa. Tourists complained they were afraid to walk our streets. My eldest daughter, who spends a good deal of time in Washington, was shocked to see the number and aggressiveness of the panhandlers during one of her infrequent forays into downtown Ottawa. "This is worse than Washington," she claimed, "and that's really saying something because Washington is hardly the centre of civility."

With the passing of the Safe Streets Act, however, almost overnight the squeegee people disappeared and police were able to hustle the hasslers away from our churches, Ottawa's Byward Market, Toronto street corners, and anywhere else where aggressive panhandling was taking place.

You would think everyone would welcome all of this. Ha! The squeegee supporters screamed bloody murder and they've been doing everything in their power ever since to have the Act repealed.

The Ontario Court of Appeal upheld the legislation in a 2001 decision, but it is still under appeal and the case will likely end up in the Supreme Court of Canada where, from all reports, many municipalities, including Toronto (Ottawa City Council thankfully voted to uphold the Act), will join with the IWW union in fighting it.

Which begs another question: Where in the heck does all the money to support these appeals come from? It is estimated that taking an appeal to the Supreme Court costs in the neighbourhood of a million dollars. Who pays for this and why? Are we taxpayers going to get stuck with the bill? We certainly will be if, in fact, our city councils join the appeal.

It's astonishing, isn't it? In New York City they started cleaning up the city and its crime and welfare problems by getting rid of the squeegee people. Here in Ontario we managed to get rid of the problem ten years ago, and ever since that time, half the province has been working hard to bring it back!

When ideology and reality meet head-on, in Canada ideology wins every time, aided and abetted in no small way by the incredible apathy of the average Canadian.

NINE

The Self-Chosen Ones

A constant thread through all these stories is the disconnect from reality displayed by many of the self-described "progressives," some of whom appear to be on some kind of holy crusade to save us from ourselves.

It is truly remarkable that many policies, multiculturalism for example, are adopted with no empirical evidence as to their necessity, desirability, practicality, or consequences. In many instances involving social policy, no opposing theories are even sought, nor is there any systemic testing of the policy after implementation.

As Thomas Sowell, Senior Fellow at the Hoover Institute, Stanford University, says, in his groundbreaking book *The Vision of the Anointed: Self-Congratulation As a Basis for Social Policy* (Basic Books, 1996): "Momentous questions are dealt with essentially as conflicts of vision." You would almost think Sowell, who is acknowledged as one of American's leading social commentators, is talking about two of the great visions we have been presented with here in Canada—multiculturalism and bilingualism.

Without arguing the merits of either, you have to admit that both of these momentous policies were presented as a vision to Canadians without study or debate. Oh, it is true we had the Royal Commission on Bilingualism and Biculturalism, launched by Prime Minister Lester Pearson in the mid 1960s, but essentially its intent was not to determine if Canada should become an officially bilingual nation but rather to justify the idea and determine how best to implement what became a defining aspect of Canadian life.

It is also a fact that even though Prime Minister Pierre Trudeau introduced the Official Languages Act in 1969, he later came to a major parting of the ways with the B and B Commission, pursuing a policy of multiculturalism rather than biculturalism.

But at no time during this long drawn-out process did we Canadians as a whole have any say in choosing the path the country took and is still taking. In fact, most attempts at even questioning the wisdom of either bilingualism or multiculturalism bring a cascade of abuse crashing down on the questioner's head. No doubt, some of you have severe headaches from this!

I have suggested upon many occasions on my radio show and in print that the policies of official bilingualism and official multiculturalism are in direct conflict with each other. It seems only common sense that the more people we bring to Canada who speak neither French nor English, the more difficult it will become to have all Canadians speak both those official languages. According to the 2002 census, there are about 130,000 people in Ottawa alone whose mother tongue is neither English nor French.

In fact, what many others and I have been trying to point out for years is absolutely true. Any of you who have visited Toronto or Vancouver recently know very well you can walk for blocks in some districts in those cities and never once hear an English or French word. There are large numbers of second- and even third-generation residents who cannot speak a word of English or French and, because they have settled in large ghettos, have no need to. This is vastly and dangerously different from immigrants who arrived only a couple of decades ago. They had to learn the local language well enough to earn a living and made very sure their children spoke it perfectly.

As for bilingualism, a grand idea no doubt, but west of the Ottawa Valley, aside from small pockets in northern Ontario and Manitoba, official bilingualism is a minor blip on the radar screen of most Canadians.

So how do these momentous social policy issues become part of the Canadian landscape? How do policies such as these become so ingrained in our society that they become the prevailing vision of so many?

Sowell, in *The Vision of the Anointed*, has an interesting theory: He says what these grand visions may offer and what the prevailing vision of our time does offer is a special state of grace for those who believe in it. "Those who accept this vision," he writes, "are deemed to be not merely factually correct but morally on a higher plane. Those who disagree are seen as being not only in error, but in sin."

Sowell calls the political and intellectual elite of our time "the anointed." The rest of us, he says, are "benighted." We do not play on the same moral ground. We are to be made "aware" have our "consciousness raised," must be "fought," and the "real reasons" behind our arguments and actions exposed.

I suspect Sowell is absolutely right, and sadly, the problem is made more severe in Canada by a largely left-wing media that seldom questions any prevailing beliefs, and the universities in the land that seem intent upon turning out graduates with a single point of view—decidedly on the Left.

All of this is fuelled by a truly incredible number of government-sponsored or subsidized think tanks and foundations, which, according to authors Tasha Kheiriddin and Adam Daifallah in their recent book *Rescuing Canada's Right: A Blueprint for a Conservative Revolution* (John Wiley & Sons, 2005), have received an astounding $9 billion in federal funding since 1997. In almost every case, these think tanks and foundations conduct studies, surveys, and polls that inevitably conclude that what the country wants and needs is more statism—that is more government in our daily lives, more social programs, and naturally, more taxes.

No matter what the cause of the day happens to be—from bilingualism to state-run daycare—a taxpayer-funded think tank or a foundation, often both, can be found to track down information and arguments to support the government's point of view. All done with our money, of course!

Two examples: Official Language organizations received $76 million between 1970 and 1982. Multicultural groups received $20 million in 1987-88 alone. [Source: Kheiriddin and Daifallah in *Rescuing Canada's Right* as cited above.]

Keep in mind the foundations, of which there could be as many as 300, aren't subject to Freedom of Information legislation or audit, so it is impossible to determine exactly how their money is spent. In short, about one billion dollars a year

of taxpayers' money pours into these think tanks and foundations, about which most Canadians know nothing.

Rather than "the anointed," I think a more accurate description of these "old white guys" making all these important decisions for us (as Conservative MP Rona Ambrose once described
them in the House of Commons) is the "self-chosen ones,"
since it is obvious that with rare exceptions we never had a
chance to choose the people who decide what vision the country shall pursue. They chose themselves! Heck, in Canada we
don't even get to choose our prime minister!

Have our two great visions—bilingualism and multiculturalism—failed?

Will they fail?

What constitutes failure? Surely francophone public servants with so little loyalty to Canada that they vote for a separatist candidate are an indication of a terrible failure of our
bilingualism policies.

Quebec almost packed it in and still may, hardly a rousing
endorsement of Canada despite our very substantial efforts to
accommodate the French fact.

Adherence, even an understanding, of traditional Canadian
values among many ethnic communities is dubious at best. Is
it multiculturalism we have in Canada, or no culture? Outside
Quebec, that is! It's interesting, isn't it, how Quebec politicians
insist that while the rest of Canada must become a nation of
dozens of different cultures, Quebec must remain distinctly
homogenous—a monoculture? It was a Quebec politician by
the name of Pierre Trudeau who told us that aside from
Quebec, we were now a multicultural nation.

Many European nations have begun to rethink and revise

their immigration policies as their national identities becomes increasingly fuzzy. Britain today realizes it made a dreadful mistake in attempting to create a multicultural society and is trying desperately to remedy it. So is Holland, which early in 2006 deported 26,000 mostly Muslims who had entered the country illegally. Should we follow suit? Would we have the courage to weather the slanderous attacks from the Left to actually do anything to remedy what is obviously a terribly failed refugee program?

I could ask a thousand questions about policies we have taken—roads we are now travelling—and the answer almost inevitably would be the same. Some of the policies seem to be working okay. With some, the jury may still be out, but with others, including some major ones, it's a total failure, either a complete disaster or quickly headed in that direction.

Chief among the shoals we are plunging towards is our vision of multiculturalism, which I believe has already begun to take Canada in a direction most of us really do not wish to go.

None of this, unfortunately, will change until our vision of what we wish Canada to be changes.

I remember a few years ago asking listeners what made them most proud to be a Canadian. It was a big mistake on my part. It made for a very dull hour, since the answers for the most part were identical. Our health care system and the fact that unlike the Americans ours is a multicultural nation, were the almost universal responses.

I suspect that today, with hospital waiting lists growing longer and the ethnic ghettos getting larger and spawning homegrown terrorists, most callers would be much more ambivalent about both those policies.

But does that mean we are ready to learn from our mistakes and go to Plan B? Not likely, at least not until things get much worse.

These two defining Canadian policies, along with health care, are just more examples of how the self-chosen ones refuse to avert disaster by changing course. Refuse to admit they have been in error. Refuse to concede, even as we are about to plunge over a cliff, that the path they are leading us along needs a slight alternation, let alone a quick jam into reverse!

Even though their solutions to the various social problems that confront us are proven time and time again to fail, those who launched them are not deterred. Indeed, the more they are proven wrong, the more they insist they are right! If their solution to crime results in higher crime rates, we are informed it is because of demographics, or racism, or, as the Governor General claimed in her speech opening the spring session of the Ontario Legislature, the criminals are driven to do their nasty deeds by "outrageous shortcomings" in society.

When the ethnic ghettos created by our state-sponsored multiculturalism programs become petri dishes of violence and hatred towards Canadian values, we are informed it's because our troops are in Afghanistan or because we disallowed sharia law.

If welfare roles double when we double welfare payments, it's because we didn't increase payments enough, sexism, racism, or some other anomaly that had absolutely nothing to do with more people taking welfare because the pay is better!

Conversely, when the welfare roles plunged by half when Mike Harris cut payments by 20 percent and introduced his "work for welfare" program, the self-chosen ones and their fellow travellers were outraged and claimed those no longer on welfare hadn't really gone back to work, but had somehow been bullied into disappearing. Just where they had disappeared to, they refuse to tell us. The fact is what happened with crime and welfare rates just isn't part of their view of the world.

When young blacks begin shooting young blacks, and by mistake the odd white person, it's not our immigration or multicultural policies that are in error, but something else, probably racism.

When Quebec comes within one half percent of voting to separate, it's not because our bilingualism or bicultural policies have failed, it's because restaurants in the Byward Market don't have French on their menus—or something!

This inability or unwillingness to accept feedback and change a course of action that is failing is very dangerous.

Mankind has always made mistakes. Always will. When we recognize and acknowledge those mistakes and adjust our course we can avert disaster. But history is littered with the shattered remnants of civilizations that have blindly continued a course of action despite all the feedback that cries out, disaster ahead! Millions of Germans could clearly see that the ride Hitler was taking them on was going to plunge them into a nightmare, but millions more bought into Hitler's dream of a super race taking over the world, and Hitler's henchmen saw to it that almost all negative feedback—all warnings of impending doom—were snuffed out.

The prevailing belief, the orthodoxy of the day in Germany, was that they could not be defeated and all the evidence in the world to the contrary was ignored. We all know the consequences!

I am not suggesting we're headed for a blitzkrieg or anything approaching it, but the evidence of moral decay and a crumbling civilization are everywhere and the protests and pleas from those of us who see the failed policies all around us fall mostly on the deaf ears of those who claim their policies have succeeded despite overwhelming evidence to the contrary. Many of those responsible for today's failed policies cannot bring themselves to even consider the possibility that their view of the world, their vision, is wrong.

The prevailing belief in Canada today is that socialism is best for us—that multiculturalism, bilingualism, and soft justice are working. Very few of us are yet ready to question whether the Left's vision of how the world works is the correct one.

You can be very sure that had Paul Martin and the Liberals not been up to their eyeballs in scandal and incompetence there is no way the Canadian public would have ever considered straying even slightly off the disastrous path we have been taking to give Stephen Harper and the Conservatives a chance to make some slight changes in direction.

The message on January 23, 2006, was very clear: Mr. Harper, don't you dare stray far off that path to the nanny state or we'll boot your sorry butt out of there mighty fast!

This path, of course, has led us to a crumbling health care system, denigration of the role of parenting, an education system failing our children badly, a military in shambles, a sieve for a border, tens of thousands of refugees ordered deported that we cannot locate, and taxes so high that today it takes two incomes for the average family to live as happily as our parents did with one income.

Family breakdown is at an all-time high, as is drug use, and HIV infection. Juvenile crime is soaring, just about everyone complains about stress, half the country breaks the law by taking part in the underground economy, and depression, they claim, has never been more severe. But, but, despite all of this and a good deal more bad news, this is the path many still maintain is the best for us. To even contemplate anything else is "scary"!

Mankind has been engaged in ideological warfare of one kind or another since the dawn of recorded history. Probably well before that. From the divine right of kings, the Magna Carta, the French Revolution, fascism, Nazism, communism, socialism, environmentalism, secularism. Always it has been a struggle for power and nothing has changed today.

It is still a fierce battle between those who believe they have superior wisdom and morality, and the rest of us, who, they believe, are sadly lacking in both wisdom and virtue.

One thing that has changed from the days of chopping off heads or machine-gunning the mob, are the methods used to exert the superiority of those who have chosen themselves as the arbiters of social justice. Today it's much subtler. Besides which, the modern socialist, unlike those who went before, has an aversion to blood.

There are four steps that must be taken to launch yet another social engineering crusade:

1. Create the appearance of a major crisis. This always comes first! It doesn't matter what kind of crisis. It can be a new invention or a retread of an old one (when the rabble tires of the cry for higher welfare payments, it suddenly becomes child poverty). Always this crisis is one that you and I just don't know about and are way too dumb to understand anyway. The media, always

looking for a story they don't have to dig for, can be counted on to headline this latest crisis until the ink runs out!

2. Set up a loud hew and cry for government action to solve the crisis before we're all stricken with a multitude of terrible disasters (poverty, AIDS, global warming, pesticides, avian flu…). Once again the media does a little two-step along with all of this. The longer the title of the expert assuring us that catastrophe lies just around the corner if we don't immediately respond to this latest crisis, the bigger the headline. By response, of course, the social engineers and their experts always mean "bury us with money."

3. Fervently lobby government to impose sufficient restrictions, rules, regulations, bans, fines, or jail terms for those of us who are creating and adding to this terrible crisis. This is always coupled with mountains of studies, armies of experts, and utter disdain for anyone who dares challenge their assertions.

4. Those who invented the crisis present themselves and their friends as the only ones with the superior wisdom required to understand and appreciate the gravity of the situation. They alone are equipped to deal with the crisis. No government could possibly resist the logic, so huge sums of money come pouring out of our pockets and thus is born unto us a multitude of committees, studies, conferences, agencies, outreach groups, safe houses, resource centres, workshops, plenary sessions… None of this in any way alleviates the crisis, because in most cases none ever existed, but it does provide won-

derful employment for multitudes of people who would otherwise be unemployable.

The best modern example of this lovely little four-step do-si-do is the creation of the greatest crisis of all time, the imminent destruction of the planet: GLOBAL WARMING!

TEN

Ice Cubes in Your Glass

We've got pretty good security here at CFRA on George Street, but somehow this guy has slipped through and is waiting for me after my show. He's wearing some kind of knitted kamikaze hat with the earflaps down, but it's his eyes that have me worried. Wild and not too well focused. I've always kind of figured a suicide bomber would take me out in the end and this looks the time and the place! But it's not a bomb he's holding. It's a glass about half filled with water and the dregs of a couple of ice cubes. He waves it under my nose with a grimy fist and shouts, "See Green, as usual you're full of s—t!" Now I know what this is all about and I start to laugh.

I take him up to the second floor where we have, for some unknown reason, a refrigerator mostly filled with two- and three-year-old lunch remnants and always in the freezer, buckets of ice cubes guarded by a crudely drawn sign that reads "Sales Department."

"Give me your glass," I say. Apprehensively, he hands it over. I half fill the glass with water, add three ice cubes, mark the level with some tape, place it on a table and point to a chair.

"How about you sit there, and leave the glass here, like this, until the ice cubes melt. Then you tell me if the water level has risen above the tape." He looks at me like I'm crazy. By this time, though, he's calmed down a bit and doesn't come right out and say so, but you can tell that he knows he's really going to show me up for the fool he knows me to be.

I should have known better. About half an hour later, when the cubes are fully melted and the water hasn't risen even a hair's breadth, his eyes go wild again. "You cheated. You're a cheap liar, Green." He grabs his glass, water splashing over the table. "Those were trick ice cubes!" Ramming his hat even more firmly over his ears, he stomps out in disgust.

• • •

It hits me suddenly as I am lying on my favourite beach on the beautiful island of Grand Bahama. Deadman's Reef is out there, just as I have seen it for the 40 years I'd been coming to this little paradise in the sun. The waves still lap the same coral outcropping I'd been parking my car on for 40 years. To exactly the same place on that rock, as a matter of fact. Which is the point.

I sit bolt upright. "Debbie," I almost shout, "they're lying to us!"

She cocks a quizzical eyebrow at me. A nearby sunbathing couple edges further away. After 25 years, my wife is used to this kind of outburst. "What now? Who's lying?"

I point to the waves gently nudging the front tires of our little rented Corolla. "Remember the first time you came here with me and how worried you were that the waves were going to wash our car away?" She sits up now, becoming more convinced that this time I have really lost it. "So? That's almost 25 years ago."

"Precisely," I say, "that's the point. Remember what I told you then?" She pauses for a moment. "You said there was nothing to worry about, it was high tide and the water never came any higher."

She is absolutely right. I'd been coming to that same beach, parking my car on that same rock for 15 years before Deborah and I met, and now 25 years after that, the water at high tide comes to almost the exact same spot it had 40 years ago! Sometimes a bit lower, sometimes a bit higher, depending upon the wind and the phase of the moon. But essentially the level of the ocean has not changed in 40 years.

"What it means,'" I say, "is that all this talk about the oceans flooding the land because of global warming is a damn lie. All the oceans of the world are linked. The Arctic Ocean can't rise without the Caribbean rising or the Pacific for that matter, so all this business about melting glaciers causing widespread flooding is just a pile of nonsense. And if they're lying about that, they're probably lying about everything else to do with global warming."

When I get back on the air a week later, I raise this issue on my show. "Listen," I say, "don't take my word for it; see for yourself. Put some ice cubes in a glass of water, mark the level of the water, let the ice melt and then see if the level of the water rises. It's Archimedes' principle," I explain, or try to. "A body immersed in a fluid is buoyed up by a force equal to the weight of the displaced fluid. They keep talking about the Arctic ice cap melting and setting the streets of Halifax and Vancouver awash, but the Arctic ice cap is all floating and when floating ice melts it doesn't raise the level of the oceans one nanometre!

It is a big mistake! I am immediately under attack from all quarters. Despite my urging to try the ice-cubes-in-the-glass "scientific" experiment, caller after caller makes it very clear I am nuts! Ditto that simple old fool Archimedes, whoever he is!

"It's got to raise the level of the water when an ice cap or iceberg melts," I am assured dozens of times by callers who try to explain to me that when all the ice which was above the water melts, it only stands to reason that it adds to the volume of the oceans, and thus they will rise. This essentially is what some scientists have been telling us as well, so it doesn't come as much of a surprise that so many people actually believe it.

This went on for several days, highlighted by the visit from our kamikaze-hatted nutcase friend, until a few people who tried the ice-cubes-in-the-glass experiment had to grudgingly admit that maybe I was right after all. Some actually seemed shocked to realize that much of what they had heard about widespread flooding was a lie.

Several callers pointed out that while it might be true that floating ice doesn't raise the ocean's level when it melts, it is a different story with land-based ice. The real danger, they claimed, is if the glaciers on Greenland begin to melt—then we are in real trouble.

So I began to check that theory out as well. Guess what? For the most part, that's also a pile of nonsense.

In the first place, about 90 percent of all the earth's ice is in Antarctica where the average temperature, depending upon which scientific group you believe, is either −37°F, −50°F or −57°F. The scientists, it turns out, can't even agree on how cold

Antarctica is. If you don't believe me, just google "average temperature in Antarctica."

Common sense tells me that if the earth's temperature shoots up to the point where the Antarctic ice begins to melt, we humans have long since become nothing more than grease spots.

Greenland, on the other hand, has only about 5 percent of the earth's ice. Even if every bit of ice on it melted and ran into the sea, it is highly unlikely it would affect the earth's oceans much more than a very heavy rainfall.

I'm not a scientist, I'm not a meteorologist, I'm not a climatologist, but I do know Archimedes' principle and I do have a bit of common sense. If the water on my beach down there in the Bahamas hasn't risen a hair's breadth in 40 years despite all the melting glaciers they keep trying to scare us with, then I suspect we're pretty safe at least until the sun begins to fry us all into crispy critters!

"Okay, maybe the bit about flooding half the world is a bit exaggerated," said one of my callers, "but what about global warming itself. Most scientists in the world agree we're headed for some kind of disaster if we humans don't sign onto the Kyoto Accord and stop producing so much smog."

"Stop right there," I told him. "In the first place, nowhere near all the scientists in the world agree either that we are confronted with anything other than a minor warming of the earth from natural causes, or that humans are responsible."

In fact, some of Canada's leading scientists and climatologists are so upset over what they feel are lies and misinformation being spread about global warming that they have formed a group they call the "Friends of Science" to question and sometimes refute information we are being fed.

ELEVEN

Are These People Nuts?

Friends of Science describe themselves as a non-profit organization made up of active and retired engineers, earth scientists, and other professionals, as well as many concerned Canadians who believe the science behind the Kyoto Protocol is questionable. Friends of Science has assembled a scientific advisory board of esteemed climate scientists from around the world to offer, as their website, www.friendsofscience.org, states, "a critical mass of current science on global climate and climate change to policy makers and any interested parties."

You may have heard some of the commercials they paid for recently on Canadian radio stations in an attempt to spark a national and international debate on global warming. They say they offer "critical evidence" that challenges the premises of the Kyoto Protocol and present alternative causes for climate change.

To counter any suspicion you may have that only fringe or kook scientists would dispute global warming and the necessity for Kyoto, let's have a close look at who is on the scientific advisory board of Friends of Science, and you tell me if they sound like crackpots!

Dr. Tim Ball, Retired Professor of Climatology, Consultant: Dr. Ball was the first Canadian PhD in Climatology. He has an extensive background in climatology, especially the reconstruction of past climates and the impact of climate change on human history and the human condition. Dr. Ball has a BA (Honours), an MA (University of Manitoba) and a PhD (Doctor of Science, University of London, England). He is currently an environmental consultant and for 32 years was Professor of Climatology at the University of Winnipeg.

Dr. Sallie Baliunas, Research scientist at the Harvard-Smithsonian Center for Astrophysics in Cambridge, Massachusetts: Dr. Baliunas serves as Senior Scientist at the George C. Marshall Institute in Washington, DC, and chairs the Institute's Science Advisory Board. She is also Visiting Professor at Brigham Young University, Adjunct Professor at Tennessee State University, and past contributing editor to the *World Climate Report*. She received her MA and PhD in Astrophysics from Harvard University.

Dr. Chris de Freitas, Associate Professor of Geography and Environmental Science, University of Auckland: Dr. de Freitas completed bachelor's and master's degrees at the University of Toronto and a PhD at the University of Queensland, Australia, as a Commonwealth Doctoral Scholar. During his time at the University of Auckland, he has served as Deputy Dean of Science, Dean of Science, Head of Science and Technology at the Tamaki Campus and spent four years as Pro Vice Chancellor. His academic interests are broad but he focuses mostly on climate. He was also a contributing reviewer to the Intergovernmental Panel on Climate Change, Scientific Assessment Reports, in 1995 and again in 2001.

Dr. Madhav L. Khandekar, Meteorologist, retired, formerly with Environment Canada: Dr. Khandekar specializes in understanding extreme weather events in Canada and in other parts of the world. He holds BSc and PhD degrees in meteorology from Florida State University. As one of the world leaders in meteorology, Dr. Khandekar has worked in the fields of climatology, meteorology, and oceanography for more than 45 years and has published nearly 100 papers, reports, book reviews, and scientific commentaries, as well as a book on ocean wave analysis and modelling.

Dr. Tad Murty, Adjunct Professor in the Department of Earth Sciences at the University of Ottawa: Dr. Murty specializes in the mathematical modelling of natural marine hazards under climate change. He holds a BSc in Physics, a MSc in meteorology, oceanography and hydrology from Indian universities, and an MS and a PhD in meteorology and oceanography from the University of Chicago. He has published more than 215 peer-reviewed articles in scientific journals and has authored, co-authored, and edited 15 books. He is also a specialist on tsunamis and is currently involved in several tsunami projects at the request of the Canadian Government. In addition to his role at the University of Ottawa, Dr. Murty is Adjunct Professor in the Department of Civil Engineering at the University of Ottawa. He is also associated with the Natural Resources Institute of the University of Manitoba.

Dr. Tim Patterson, Professor of Geology and Paleoclimatology, Carleton University: Dr. Tim Patterson received both a BSc in biology and a BA in geology from Dalhousie University in Halifax, and a PhD in geology from the University of California. He is Canadian leader of the

International Geological Correlation Program Project IGCP 495 "Quaternary Land-Ocean Interactions" and is principle investigator of a Canadian Foundation for Climate and Atmospheric Science project studying high-resolution Holocene climate records from anoxic fjords and coast lakes in British Columbia.

What do you think? Does that sound like a slate of kooks or wackos? Hardly!

TWELVE

How Hot Is It?

The following is some of what Friends of Science have to say on their website about global warming and Kyoto:

> Accurate satellite, balloon, and mountain-top observations made over the last three decades have not shown any significant change in the long-term rate of increase in global temperatures. Average ground station readings do show a mild warming of 0.6° to 0.8°C over the last 100 years. This is well within the natural variations recorded in the last millennium. The ground station network suffers from an uneven distribution across the globe: The stations are preferentially located in growing urban and industrial areas (heat islands) which show substantially higher readings than adjacent rural areas.
>
> There has been no catastrophic warming recorded.

Concerning the so-called "hockey stick" graph which some say proves that the earth's temperature (which increased gradually over a thousand years) has recently begun to shoot up—here is what the Friends of Science have to say:

> Significant changes in climate have continually occurred throughout geologic time. For instance, the Medieval Warm Period, from about 1000 to 1200 AD (when the Vikings farmed on Greenland) was followed by a period know as the Little Ice Age. Since the end of the 17th century, the average global temperature has been rising at

the low steady rate mentioned, although from 1940 to 1970 temperatures actually dropped leading to a global cooling scare.

The "hockey stick" graph is a poster boy of both the United Nations' and IPPC Canada's Environment Department ignore historical recorded climatic swings, and has now also been proven to be flawed and statistically unreliable as well. It is a computer construct and a faulty one at that.

One of the claims often made by supporters of Kyoto is that human-produced carbon dioxide has increased drastically over the last 100 years and is a major cause of the greenhouse effect, thus warming the planet.

The Friends of Science say carbon dioxide (CO_2) levels have indeed changed for various reasons, human and otherwise, just as they have throughout geologic time. Say the Friends:

Since the beginning of the industrial revolution the CO_2 content of the atmosphere has increased from a rate of about 0.2 percent per year to the present 0.1 percent per year. But there is no proof that CO_2 is the main driver of global warming. As measured in ice cores dated over many thousands of years, CO_2 levels move up and down after the temperature has done so and thus are the result of, not the cause of warming. Geological field work in recent sediments confirms this causal relationship.

The Friends then go on to say:

There is solid evidence that as temperatures move up and down naturally and cyclically, through solar radiation, orbital and galactic influences, the warming surface layers of the earth's oceans expel more CO_2 as a result.

The Friends of Science also dispute the claim that CO_2 is the most common greenhouse gas. They claim that greenhouse gases form about 3 percent of the atmosphere by volume. The atmosphere consists of varying amounts (about 97 percent) of water vapour and clouds, with the remainder being gases such as CO_2, CH_4, Ozone, and N_2O of which carbon dioxide is the largest amount. Hence CO_2 constitutes about 0.037 percent of the atmosphere. Water vapour and clouds are responsible for 60 percent of the greenhouse effect."

Dr. Tad Murty, who has been a guest on my show on CFRA several times, says one of his main concerns about the Kyoto Accord is that it deals almost exclusively with carbon dioxide and not the kind of pollution that we see in smog, or water pollution for that matter.

Says Dr. Murty, "Instead of spending billions on the junk science behind Kyoto, we should instead be spending the money cleaning up real pollution—in our air and water." He points out, as well, that if just a tiny fraction of the money we are spending on Kyoto had instead been directed to building a tsunami early-warning system, as he recommended years ago, thousands of lives could have been saved in the terrible Boxing Day tsunami in Southeast Asia.

"Many people," he says, "believe that Kyoto is about ridding ourselves of smog and other forms of air pollution. Nothing could be further from the truth. Carbon dioxide, which is what Kyoto deals with almost exclusively, is an odourless, colourless gas that is the lifeblood of all living plants on earth. Lowering CO_2 emissions will in no way lessen real pollution, in the air or water."

I asked Dr. Tim Ball, when he was my guest on the CFRA noon hour "Lunch Bunch" program, a direct question: "Do you believe it is even possible for mankind to affect the earth's climate?" Without hesitation, he replied emphatically, "No!"

Dr. Ball concludes his website comments with this thought: "Canadians must hold extremists to account and ask why they seek to play magistrate and exclude legitimate climate scientists from the debate. Do they consider themselves gods? Or is it just that their stance is so weak they fear a truly open discussion?"

No mincing of words there!

THIRTEEN

The Green Zealots

Recently, in a blistering recent letter to the editor of the *Financial Post*, Dr. Tim Ball wrote: "Canada could lead the world out of the mess we have been led into by zealous and uninformed green activists. At the very least, we will need to deal with the fallout when the public realize how much they have been hoodwinked, exploited, and made to pay a huge unnecessary cost, or their reaction will be to place science and scientists in as low a category as politicians!"

The whole thrust to claim global warming is an impending disaster caused primarily by humans began with a report issued by the United Nations Intergovernmental Panel of Climate Change in 1996, acting on recommendations made at the 1992 Rio Summit (more about Rio later).

It has been widely reported that the panel claimed that human activity was responsible for greenhouse gas that was warming the planet. Gradually, however, the truth is coming to light.

According to the Friends of Science, the UN report was deliberately altered and two key statements deleted in the final report.

Those two statements are as follows:

1. None of the studies cited above has shown clear evidence that we can attribute the observed climate changes to increases in greenhouse gases; and

2. No study to date has positively attributed all or part of the climate change to man-made causes.

The Friends of Science say those two sentences were deliberately deleted from the final report and that to the present day there is still no scientific proof that man-made CO_2 causes significant global warming.

Dr. John Christy, a professor of atmospheric science and director of the Earth System Center at the University of Alabama, who was the lead author of the UN report, has verified this.

Dr. Christy says the public must be made aware of the fact that most of the scientists involved with the panel do not agree that global warming is occurring. The findings of the panel, he says, have been consistently misrepresented and/or politicized with each succeeding report. Dr. Christy's latest paper, published in the *Journal of Atmospheric and Oceanic Technology*, says atmospheric estimates of global warming "show much less warming than first reported, less than half observed at the surface. The real world shows less warming in the atmosphere, not more, as models predict."

He told a US congressional committee hearing that computer models related to global warming "should be viewed with great skepticism."

So why all the scare tactics? Good question.

My grandfather always told me any time I was confronted with something I couldn't understand to just "follow the money."

If you do that in this case, you'll find that there's a lot of money to be made by a lot of people with this whole Kyoto thing. Many scientists doing all the warning are making a good living at it, as are the professional scaremongers getting paid to frighten the bejabbers out of us, but probably the biggest issue of all is this whole business of carbon credits.

It's a little hard to understand, but Kyoto is mostly about transferring gobs of money from wealthy nations like Canada to poorer nations like China and some Third World states in Africa and South America. The idea is that instead of Canada having to reduce its carbon dioxide emissions (lowering them to Kyoto standards would bankrupt half the businesses in Canada), we could buy so-called carbon credits from countries like China, which are so poorly developed they aren't producing much CO_2. Believe it or not, carbon-credit brokers have already set up shop, and from some reports have already begun to do some business with Chile.

But there's probably more to it than just money. Here again we discover our old friend—left-wing ideology.

During his testimony before the Congressional Committee, Doctor Christy said:

> The global warming hoax is not about the Earth's climate. It is about an attack on the economics of those nations that produce much of the world's wealth. Our country [the US] is often criticized for producing 25 percent of the world's anthropogenic CO_2; however, we are rarely recognized and applauded for producing, with that same CO_2, 31 percent of what the world wants and needs: its food, technology, medical advances, defence of freedom and so on.

He continued:

The industrialized nations of the world are the target of the environmentalists. By every means possible they have sought to undermine economic growth and to enhance the reduction of human life on this planet. Those of us who defend growth are assailed as tools of multinational corporations and advocates for pollution. Nothing could be further from the truth.

Dr. Christy went on to say:

Carbon dioxide is not a pollutant. In simple terms CO_2 is the lifeblood of the planet. The vegetation we see around us would disappear, if not for atmospheric CO_2. This green world largely evolved during a period when the atmospheric CO_2 concentration was many times what it is today; in other words, carbon dioxide means life itself.

Dr. Christy's claim that the Kyoto movement is mostly about attacking the industrialized nations of the world and slowing growth is dismissed by many. And yet! Read on...

FOURTEEN

Custodian of the Planet

New Yorker magazine once declared, "The survival of civilization in something like its present form might depend significantly on the efforts of a single man." The *New York Times* has hailed that same man as "Custodian of the Planet!"

The man is Maurice Strong, generally acknowledged as the father of the Kyoto Accord.

Never heard of him? That's one of the great mysteries about the man. Surely no Canadian has ever accomplished as much, has had as much worldwide influence, been as controversial, and had such a low public profile as Maurice Strong.

Among the hats he wears or has worn are: Senior Advisor to UN Secretary General Kofi Annan and Under Secretary General of the UN; Senior Advisor to World Bank President James Wolfensohn; Chairman of the Earth Council; Chairman of the Word Resources Institute; Co-chairman of the Council of the World Economic Forum; member of Toyota's International Advisory Board; UN Special Envoy in negotiations with North Korea over nuclear weapons, and that's only a start.

By the time he was 35, Strong was executive vice-president of Power Corporation of Canada and has, according to his own biography *Where on Earth Are We Going?* (Texere, 2001, Foreword by Kofi Annan), made considerable sums of money in the oil business.

In 1966, Strong launched the Canadian International Development Agency (CIDA), became president of the YMCA of Canada, and was invited by then UN Secretary General U Thant to organize what became the first Earth Summit—the Conference on the Human Environment held in Stockholm in 1972. It was at this conference that Strong first began a campaign, which eventually led to Kyoto, claiming that if the world's population and pollution weren't drastically reduced, we were facing what I would call a "doomsday scenario." (See Strong's article "The Stockholm Conference," part 1 of the article "Human Environment: The Impending Crisis" by Maurice Strong, R.P. Verney and N.A. Iliff in *The Geographical Journal*, December 1972.)

In 1975, Strong was invited back to Canada by Prime Minister Trudeau to head up Petro-Canada, and thereafter was appointed by Ontario Premier Bob Rae to be CEO of Ontario Hydro.

In 1983, Strong was appointed to the UN's World Commission on Environment and Development (the Brundtland Commission) headed by Dr. Gro Harlem Brundtland, leader of Norway's Labour Party, avowed socialist since the age of seven and Norwegian Prime Minister on three separate occasions. It was during his tenure on the Brundtland Commission that Maurice

Strong proposed and then organized the 1992 United Nations Conference on Environment and Development in Rio de Janeiro, Brazil (UNCED). Also known as the Rio Summit or just Rio, UNCED brought together 118 heads of state and over 100,000 individuals to discuss the future of the planet. It was the largest, most complex UN conference ever held, and it was at this conference that Kyoto was born, all under Maurice Strong's guiding hand.

At the opening session of the Rio Summit, Strong told the audience (found at http://www.sovereignty.net/p/sd/strong. html) that industrialized countries have:

> ...developed and benefited from the unsustainable patterns of production and consumption which have produced our present dilemma. It is clear that current lifestyles and consumption patterns of the affluent middle class—involving high meat intake, consumption of large amounts of frozen and convenience foods, use of fossil fuels, appliances, home and work place air conditioning and suburban housing are not sustainable. A shift is necessary toward lifestyles less geared to environmentally damaging consumption patterns.

In addition to his deeply held views about population growth, the environment, capitalism, and Western industrialized nations, Strong is also a firm believer in the "global governance" movement. In fact, he has served on the UN-funded Commission on Global Governance, which has presented to the UN a detailed plan on how to achieve a worldwide government overriding all national governments.

Strong's support for the movement is revealed in an introduction he wrote for the book *Beyond Interdependence: The Meshing of the World's Economy and the Earth's Ecology*, written by Jim MacNeill, Pieter Winsemius and Taizo Yakushiji (Oxford University Press, 1991). In it, he says: "Strengthening the role the United Nations can play will require serious exam-ination of the need to extend into the international arena the rule of law and the principle of taxation to finance agreed actions which provide the basis for governance at the national level. But this will not come about easily. Resistance to such changes is deeply entrenched."

As you can imagine, statements such as this have raised the hackles of more than a few people.

Noted Canadian author Elaine Dewar told me she inter-viewed Maurice Strong extensively for her book *Cloak of Green* (Lorimar and Co., 1995). "There is no doubt he is a socialist," she told me (in 1976, he told *Maclean's* magazine that he was "a socialist in ideology, a capitalist in methodology"), "and he very much wants to radically change the world."

How much he wants to change the world and how he would like to accomplish this are a matter of great conjecture. Because of the tremendous difficulty in separating fact from fiction and invention, I asked my listeners if any of them could provide me with any information concerning Mr. Strong which I might have missed. I received literally hundreds of sub-missions, almost all of which I was already aware of, but some-thing very intriguing did crop up which opens an entirely new field of questions:

Brian McAdam called in to the show. "The secret behind Kyoto is China," he said. "No nation on earth stands to gain as much through the implementation of Kyoto as does China!" Intrigued, I asked him to provide me with more information.

It turns out that Brian McAdam is a former foreign service bureaucrat who ran Canada's immigration office in Hong Kong from 1968 to 1971 and again from 1989 to 1993. He is quoted in the feature article "Puppets of Beijing" that appeared in the May 30, 2005 edition of the *Western Standard*, an article that talks about Chinese influence peddling and intelligence gathering in Canada and the United States, including large donations by Chinese agents to the Bill Clinton presidential campaign. McAdam was a key figure in a joint CSIS and RCMP investigation called Sidewinder in Canada and Chinagate in the US. The article goes into considerable detail and makes some very serious charges against a number of leading Canadians. Whether any of the claims made in the article are valid, I have no way of determining, but to my knowledge the story has not been challenged.

And let's keep something else in mind. Despite having one of the world's most powerful and burgeoning economies, Canada ships off $50 million a year in foreign aid to China; almost a million dollars a week! (Let's hope Stephen Harper puts a quick stop to this!)

What is absolutely true is that no country stands to gain as much through the implementation of Kyoto as China.

As the same *Western Standard* article claims, the Kyoto Accord, while forcing Western countries such as Canada to lower greenhouse gases to the point of curbing industrial growth, exempts China, even though it is one of the world's biggest polluters because of its massive coal-burning industries. Not only that, but because it is classed as having an underdeveloped economy, China can sell offset credits, that is, greenhouse gas allowances it doesn't use to regulated nations such as Canada for millions, perhaps billions of dollars. Under Kyoto, Canada can also gain greenhouse credits through a process called joint implementation. This is where

Canada pays to build power plants in countries like China.

When Jean Chrétien signed on to Kyoto, he stated that Canada would utilize offset credits and joint implementation strategies to meet our targets. Not only does China stand to gain billions through these two strategies, but also Chinese industries—unaffected by Kyoto limitations—can gain even more competitive advantage over their Western peers.

"Now," says Brian McAdam, "please keep in mind that Maurice Strong is not only the chief architect of the Kyoto Accord, but he has very strong ties to China and, in fact, now spends a good deal of his time in that nation!"

I have spent weeks trying to find out as much as I can about this truly amazing man, and everything I have learned makes me more convinced than ever that Kyoto has far more to do with ideology than the environment.

FIFTEEN

It's in the Stars

Yet another high-profile scientist to join the chorus of skepticism concerning global warming is prominent University of Ottawa science professor Jan Veizer who says stars, not greenhouse gases, are changing the earth's climate.

In an *Ottawa Citizen* front-page story on March 16, 2006, the professor (recently retired but still holding a research chair and still supervising grad students and postdoctoral fellows) says high-energy rays from distant parts of space are smashing into our atmosphere in ways that make our planet go through the kind of warm and cool cycles we have had for millions of years. "Cosmic rays are hitting us all the time," he says. "This has been known for a long time, but what is new is that there is now research which indicates the effects these rays are having on our world and its weather."

In 2005, *Proceedings of the Royal Society* (a major science journal in Britain) published a theory that cosmic rays form clouds and affect our climate. Today, Florida Tech and the University of Florida are investigating whether cosmic rays are the trigger that makes a charged thundercloud let rip with lightening, and a couple of years ago, scientists at NASA and the University of Kansas suggested that cosmic rays influence cloud formation, which can affect climate.

As it turns out, Professor Veizer has had doubts about greenhouse gases causing global warming for several years, but he held back because he frankly admits he was worried about the reaction from those who believe humans are causing global warming.

Until recently, anyone who dared question the greenhouse gas theory or the necessity for Kyoto was written off as some kind of crackpot or in the pay of big business.

Nonetheless, Professor Veizer finally decided to speak out and published his theory about cosmic rays in *Geoscience Canada*, the journal of the Geological Association of Canada. The article is called "Celestial Climate Driven: A Perspective from Four Billion Years of the Carbon Cycle."

In his paper, the professor concludes: "Empirical observations on all the time scales point to celestial phenomena as the principal driver of climate, with greenhouse gases acting only as potential amplifiers."

Just so no one is tempted to write Jan Veizer off as some dupe of the oil companies, let me point out that his research has been carried out over a period of many years while teaching at the University of Ottawa with no affiliation with any segment of big business. As he says, he's only going where the data he has uncovered leads him, and finally he's decided to go public with his findings.

And let's examine exactly who this man is and what his qualifications are. In 1992, Professor Jan Veizer won the Gottfried Wilhelm Leibniz Prize worth $2.2 million. It represents

Germany's highest prize for research in any field. The judges said he has "in front of his eyes the overall picture of the earth during its entire 4.5 billion years of evolution, he is one of the most creative geologists of his time." The Royal Society of Canada has called him "one of the most creative, innovative, and productive geoscientists of our times."

He was the director of the Earth System Evolution Program of the Canadian Institute of Advanced Research and held a special research chair at the University of Ottawa.

As with the scientists involved with Friends of Science, Professor Jan Veizer is hardly a wacko!

He says he feels uncomfortable with the theory that high levels of carbon dioxide alone are causing hot spells. For one thing, he says, Earth would have needed vastly more carbon dioxide than is available today to change temperatures in the manner in which they have fluctuated so much over the life span of the planet. For another, his reading of the graphs shows that some rises in carbon dioxide came *after* increases in temperature, not before. This observation corresponds with the assertions of the Friends of Science. And he says that at one time in history we appear to have had a very high carbon dioxide level during a very cold period—an icehouse, not a greenhouse!

One of the most disturbing aspects of Jan Veizer's revelations is that he admits he was scared to speak up for many years out of fear of what fellow scientists would do. Can you imagine? One of the world's leading geoscientists afraid to disagree with those who preach the greenhouse gas theory. As he says, it's a good way to start a nasty personal fight in the science world. To which I say—some world! A world where once again we see that anyone—even someone so highly qualified—who dares challenge the vision of the "self-chosen ones" is vilified, even to the point of character assassination!

When you understand what is happening here you get a much better understanding of how it is that the left-wing agenda continues to dominate social policy in this country. Challenging their agenda can get you labelled as a wacko, a racist, a pawn of big business, or worse.

SIXTEEN

Oh, My Gosh…Global Cooling?!

How about this, for heaven's sake?! The September 2006 edition of *New Scientist* magazine is warning us that what we really may be facing is GLOBAL COOLING!

Can you believe it?

The article by science writer Stuart Clark, entitled "Will the Sun Come to Our Rescue?" chronicles the findings of a group of leading scientists who warn us that there will be a new wave of global cooling because of a declining number of sunspots.

According to the scientists Clark quotes, temperature variations are largely determined by changes in solar activity. The more sunspots the warmer temperatures become on earth. Conversely, the fewer sunspots the cooler the temperatures down here become. Nigel Weiss, a solar physicist at the University of Cambridge, says it's a "boom-bust system" with the sun, and we are due for a bust very soon.

Last month, the Russian Academy of Sciences' astronomical observatory reported that global cooling could begin as early as

2012 and last for 50 years and could cool earth down to the level reached during the "little ice age" in the 17th century.

In his article, Clark notes also that only about 200 years earlier than that, a sharp downturn in temperatures turned fertile Greenland into a largely ice-covered land.

"A couple of years ago, I would not have said that there was any evidence for solar activity driving temperatures on Earth," says Paula Reimer, a palaeoclimatology expert at Queen's University, Belfast, and a source for Stuart Clark's article. "Now I think there is fairly convincing evidence."

What has won the support of Reimer and others, says Clark, is evidence linking climate to sunspots. These blemishes on the sun's surface appear and fade over days, weeks or months, depending on their size. More than a mere curiosity, they are windows on the sun's mood. Fewer sunspots pop up when the sun is calm, and historically, these periods have coincided with mini ice ages.

The number of sunspots and solar magnetic activity in general normally waxes and wanes in cycles lasting around 11 years, but every 200 years or so, the sunspots all but disappear as solar activity slumps.

According to Leif Svalgaard from Stanford University in California, who has been forecasting solar activity for nearly 30 years and who is quoted in Clark's article, we can expect a crash in sunspot activity any time now. He says that the sun's polar field is now at its weakest since measurements began in the early 1950s and that the latest figures indicate that the sun's activity will be weaker during the next decade than it has been for more than 100 years.

Interestingly enough, according to Clark, some Russian

scientists have concluded that a slight cool-down has already begun in their country.

Stay tuned, folks. As Alice would say: "It gets curiouser and curiouser…"

SEVENTEEN

The Real Poop on Polar Bears!

For several years we have been warned that global warming threatens the polar bear population with extinction. This draws many more adherents into the "Chicken Little, the sky is falling" camp, since there are some amongst us who, while caring hardly a sniff for their fellow man, go absolutely berserk at the thought of any harm befalling an animal. Besides which, if you aren't confronted with one testing your arm for flavour and tenderness, polar bears look awfully cute on the front cover of *National Geographic*.

So you can just imagine the howls of protest from the southern "climate experts" and "theorists" when the Nunavut Government, on January 1, 2005, announced a 28 percent increase in the quota allowed for hunting polar bears.

For the next year at least, hunters will be allowed to kill 518 of the bears annually, the same quota that existed between 1992 and 1996.

Simon Awa, Deputy Minister of the Environment for Nunavut, says "There were too many polar bears in the Davis Straight area for their own good." The previous fall, 628 polar bears were tagged in the area in only 90 days, and during the past several years local residents have been reporting increasing numbers of polar bears, especially near communities.

Mr. Awa says times are good for the polar bears of Davis Straight right now, thanks to an abundant supply of ring and harp seals. He goes on to say, "Polar bears have persisted through climate change cycles for millennia, as we have as Inuit hunters. People all around the world have hysteria. The reaction has been that the polar bears are going to disappear. I totally disagree with that. As a hunter, as an Inuk, I have first-hand knowledge." Referring to those who claim the polar bears will be virtually wiped out by global warming, Mr. Awa replies. "It's just one of those scare tactics."

The reaction of some of the non-Inuk to all of this is fascinating. Dr. Paul Watts, a behavioural ecologist who has spent years studying polar bears in Canada and Norway, is a contributor to a report researched and written by science writer James Hrynyshyn entitled *Chemistry, Calibre and Climate: The Plight of Canada's Polar Bear* (Canadian Marine Environment Protection Society, August 2005, page 5). In the report, Watts recognizes that Inuit hunters have been seeing some "fairly dramatic changes [increases] in polar bear prevalence." However, Watts and other scientists argue that the observations don't justify increasing the quotas.

Ian Stirling of the Canadian Wildlife Service, described as a leading expert on polar bears, says we shouldn't rely on traditional knowledge alone, but Mitch Taylor, Nunavut's chief polar bear researcher, in a 12-page report to the US Fish and Wildlife Service, says science, along with local knowledge, was taken into account before the quota was increased.

Mr. Taylor was responding to a 154-page petition from a number of conservation groups around the world demanding that polar bears be added to the list of threatened species under the US Endangered Species Act. He points out that polar bears have adapted to many environmental changes in the more than 250,000 years they have existed and that, in fact, warmer temperatures might actually increase their food supply. "There is absolutely no evidence that polar bears won't survive climate change," he says, and adds, "If polar bears are at risk, all species around the world are threatened."

It's a classic case of theory versus reality. The global warming theory is that melting ice caps will deprive polar bears of food, thus virtually wiping them out. The perfect scare tactic! The real experts—the ones who live amongst the bears—say that theory is nonsense, the bears are doing very well, thank you very much, perhaps too well for their own good. That's the reality, but as we have seen time and time again, when theory is up against reality, the theory usually wins out, no matter how wrong it may be.

It all sounds to me a little bit like the government experts who once told my father that their research proved beyond all doubt that Danish Landrace hogs wouldn't be able to adapt to the Canadian climate, even as they had already begun to revolutionize the hog industry of Canada. Today you'd be hard pressed to find a pig in Canada that doesn't have Landrace blood flowing through its veins. The hogs, totally oblivious to the experts' theories, adapted very well to Canada!

In other words, if the Inuit of Nunavut who live with them say they're being overrun with polar bears, I'm inclined to believe them rather than the government experts with their graphs, computers, and theories.

I once received an email from an irate listener who claimed I was too stupid to understand that already the polar bear population had fallen to below 1,000 and were drowning by the score as the ice cap melted at such a furious pace they could no longer swim between floes to catch their prey. "They are starving and drowning even as I write this," she fumed.

According to the Committee on the Status of Endangered Wildlife in Canada (COSEWIC) and Polar Bear International, there are between 22,000 and 27,000 polar bears in the world today. Of that figure, the Canadian government estimates 15,000 live in Canada (all figures are 1997). COSEWIC says the population of polar bears is considered to be stable and presents "a relatively low level of concern."

It's obvious these magnificent white descendents of the grizzly have become the "poster bear" of the global-warming crowd. So-called conservationists around the world are making a truly incredible number of claims about their existence and their fate, in most cases with absolutely no knowledge or understanding of conditions in the north or how polar bears might be affected.

Meantime those who live in the north, men and women whose ancestors studied every nuance of climate and wildlife in order to survive the world's most hostile environment, say the polar bears are increasing in numbers.

Some of our government "experts" claim we should not be relying on traditional knowledge alone. Oh, really? What do they think the Inuit relied on for generations? And just exactly what kind of scientific government knowledge should we rely on? The kind that administers our native Indian reserves? How about the expert scientific knowledge that advised us to buy those British submarines, or perhaps the expertise that set up and ran the Long Gun Registry!

I don't know about you, but if we're dealing with a situation in the Arctic, I'll take the kind of traditional knowledge of the people who live, work, and hunt there over some half-baked theory from some city-dwelling researcher with his computers and his charts.

Science also claims that bees, technically, should not be able to fly!

EIGHTEEN

A Climate of Fear

If they aren't trying to scare the bejabbers out of us with polar bears then it's the weather! If I want to light up my phone lines during my radio show all I have to do is suggest that hurricanes in the Bahamas, floods in Mississippi, and droughts in the Sahara have nothing to do with global warming.

A typical reaction would be one I received shortly after Katrina ripped through New Orleans. "As usual, Green, you're a damn fool," fumed the caller, "Why don't you do some research? Of course all these hurricanes and the crazy weather we're having around here are caused by global warming. It's guys like you who are causing all the problems!" Bang! Down goes the phone in my ear!

If what he said was true it would be a great relief. Instead of spending billions to lower CO_2 emissions, all the world would have to do is get rid of guys like me. I'm certain there would be plenty of volunteers!

But let's take this guy's advice and do a bit of research. Let's start with the one thing about which there seems to be general agreement. That is that global temperatures have risen about 0.6°C in the past 100 to 130 years. Which begs a very important question: How in the world can a temperature increase of less than one degree in the past century cause any kind of weather or environmental disaster? Besides which, Dr. Tad Murty, who has spent the past 20 years researching hurricanes and cyclones, says that, in fact, a close examination of records indicates that the incidence of weather catastrophes has remained more or less constant for the last half century. The difference today, he says, is that we have news and weather channels that rush to the scene of serious storms making it appear they are much more prevalent.

The record seems to bear out what Dr. Murty has to say.

The US Weather Service lists Katrina as the third-deadliest hurricane to hit the United States in the past 50 years, but eight of the other nine deadliest occurred prior to 1940. The worst recorded hurricane to hit the United States struck Galveston, Texas, on September 8, 1900, killing between 8,000 and 12,000 people and wiping out 12 city blocks. The second deadliest storm struck the Lake Okeechobee area of Florida in 1928, killing 1,836. The most intense storm ever recorded in the US was the infamous Labour Day hurricane that tore through the Florida Keys in 1935. It recorded an amazing 26.35 inches of barometric pressure at landfall.

The worst period for serious storms was actually between 1900 and 1926, when no fewer than six of the ten worst storms of the century struck the US mainland.

While there is no question that 2005 was one of the worst years on record for the number of hurricanes, there were just as many category 3 hurricanes back in 1961, and interestingly enough, the number of hurricanes recorded in 2002 and 2003 were below average while 2004 had an average number.

Hardly an indication of catastrophic climatic change!

· · ·

Early last year, one of the world's leading hurricane experts, Chris Landsea, angrily withdrew from working on a report by the Intergovernmental Panel on Climate Change (IPCC) because prominent members of the panel claimed hurricanes and global warming were clearly linked. Landsea, then with the Hurricane Research Division of the National Oceanic and Atmospheric Administration in Miami, insisted that evidence strongly suggested the impact of global warming on hurricanes is small. The recent series of bad hurricanes, he says, is just part of a natural cycle.

Landsea, in his letter of resignation, said: "I cannot in good faith continue to contribute to a process that I view as both becoming motivated by preconceived agendas and being scientifically unsound."

The link between hurricanes and global warming is also questioned in a recent article published in Geophysical Research letters.

But perhaps the most telling arguments come from Richard S. Lindzen, the Alfred P. Sloan Professor of Atmospheric Science at MIT.

In a recent *Wall Street Journal* article, highly critical of what he says are outright lies and junk science being spread by fear mongers, Professor Lindzen had this to say:

> Those who make the most outlandish claims of alarm are actually demonstrating skepticism of the very science they say supports them. It isn't just that the alarmists are trumpeting model results that we know must be wrong. It is that they

are trumpeting catastrophes that couldn't happen even if the models were right as justifying costly policies to try and prevent global warming.

If the models are correct, global warming reduces the temperature differences between the poles and the equator. When you have less difference in temperature, you have less excitation of extratropical storms, not more.

… Alarmists have drawn some support for increased claims of tropical storminess from a casual claim by Sir John Houghton of the UN's Intergovernmental Panel on Climate Change (IPCC) that a warmer world would have more evaporation with latent heat providing more energy for disturbances. The problem with this is that the ability of evaporation to drive tropical storms relies not only on temperature but humidity as well and calls for drier, less humid air. Claims for starkly higher temperature are based upon there being more humidity, not less—hardly a case for more storminess with global warming!

Professor Lindzen says the reason more scientists are not speaking up to challenge the "junk science" is that many of his colleagues have been cowed not merely by money but by fear. He goes through a list of scientists around the world who after speaking up in opposition to global warming theory have either lost government grants or in some cases their jobs. He concludes his article by saying, "Alarm, rather than genuine scientific curiosity, it appears, is essential to maintaining funding. And only the most senior scientists today can stand up against this alarmist gale and defy the iron triangle of climate scientists, advocates and policy makers." (If you would like to do your own research and read Professor Lindzen's entire article, visit http://www.opinionjournal.com/extra/?id=110008220)

Of all the things I have read, I have concluded that no one can top this assessment of Kyoto: "At the heart of the accord is a garbled anti-development urge steeped in quasi-mystical apocalyptic beliefs and which clings to the nonsensical notion that the route to helping the Third World lies in hobbling the

First." This description is written by Peter Foster in the May 24, 2006 edition of the *National Post*.

Wow!!

NINETEEN

Ottawa—a Great Place for a Dump!

I'm sitting there in a blinding snowstorm, awaiting green for go, when a rude little song my father used to delight us with when we were kids comes dancing into my head: "Oh, he stuffed his nose up a billy goat's bum and the stink would nearly blind you!" And I'm saying to myself, this is absolutely crazy. We're building a monument here to stupidity and short-sightedness which stinks so bad even a billy goat would be mortally embarrassed.

It's bad enough I've got to drive past what I've dubbed the Carp Mountain each morning, but now, just to ensure motorists are driven totally nuts, Ottawa City Council has erected a traffic light at the confluence of the most obnoxious of the fumes. When I suggest to one of our councillors that making anyone stop within a mile of the Carp Mountain, let alone at its doorstep, is surely cruel and unusual punishment, I am assured the red delay is only 90 seconds. The good councillor can apparently hold his breath for the full 90 seconds and still maintain a heart beat and is surprised I cannot.

Wait a minute, I can hear you say, what's wrong with driving by or stopping near a mountain? Good question. Unless I give you the answer. Which is that this is not your standard postcard mountain. No Lake Louise abuts its base! This is a mountain of garbage. The worst kind of garbage—other people's garbage! Trucked in daily to the west end of the Capital of Canada by giant 18-wheelers from as far away as Kingston, Belleville, and Trenton. A garbage mountain within sight and smell of Scotiabank Place, home of my beloved Ottawa Senators. A garbage mountain now at least ten stories deep, 40 stories high, (higher every day, in every way!) A city block wide and 1.1 kilometres long. Just to make matters worse, in the spring of 2006 comes news they want to more or less triple the size of this monstrosity!

The Carp Mountain—an Everest in progress—another perfect monument to our inability to learn from either our mistakes or the successes of others.

And here I have to blame the hard Left environmentalists who have somehow been able to convince most Canadians that modern methods of garbage disposal, methods used for decades in many European cities, are more dangerous than piling it into mountains.

The propaganda campaign against high-efficiency incineration, which is the method commonly used throughout Europe, began when Bob Rae, as Premier of Ontario, in response to a terrific lobbying effort by the environmentalists, banned all incineration in Toronto. Instead, they began to truck it all the way to Michigan. Somehow we were persuaded that 140 to 180 18-wheeled trucks plowing up and down the 401 each day to Michigan and back was better for the environment that incineration.

Today, some argue that we've got to be fair and admit that incineration technology in the late 1980s was not as advanced as it is today and there were problems with emissions. There is some truth to that, but it is also a fact that Sweden has been using incinerators to burn their garbage and create energy since the 1970s with no problems with emissions or pollution of any kind.

The stigma against incineration in Canada is only beginning to abate today as the public wakes up to what's happening in the world around us. But even today left-wing Toronto Mayor David Miller is still opposed to incineration as are many environmental organizations, including the Sierra Club.

I recall vividly Rod Muir, whose title is Waste Disposal Campaigner for the Sierra Club of Canada, calling my show on February 22, 2006, during the height of the controversy over the Carp Mountain, to claim that as far as his organization was concerned incineration, even high-efficiency incineration, was just as bad as piling it into heaps in our cities!

For inclusion in this book, I submitted three written questions to Mr. Muir concerning the Sierra Club's position on modern high-efficiency incineration:

Question # 1: What has the Sierra Club done to investigate and promote modern methods of waste disposal?

Response: "The short answer is nothing."

Question # 2 : Would the Sierra Club support incineration for that portion of garbage that cannot be recycled?

Response: "I am prepared to consider it."

Question # 3: Would the Sierra Club support incineration of the existing landfill sites?

Repose: "I would be greatly surprised if the energy cost of

getting at the material was outweighed by what little energy value it had and the cost to capture it."

I am astonished that Mr. Muir expresses no concern whatsoever over the environmental damage from garbage dumps. His only concern in this matter seems to be cost. He doubts if you could recover sufficient energy to cover the cost of burning it. No mention of the environmental cost that will be with us for generations. I am astounded, to say the least!

Also, please note, I asked Mr. Muir for the Sierra Club's stance on these various issues. Without exception, he responds in the first person. I asked for the Club's official position but received what appear to be the personal views of Rod Muir!

Gilles Chasles, a Stittsville businessman and a key figure in organizing opposition to tripling the size of the Carp Mountain, tells me it has been a lonely battle at times, with absolutely no support or assistance of any kind from anyone in the environmental movement. For example, on April 6, 2006, he sent the following email to an organization called the Ottawa Riverkeeper:

> I am very curious as to why we haven't heard anything from your group concerning the proposed expansion of the Carp Road Dump by Waste Management.
>
> Are you not concerned about the leachate infiltrating the watershed in and around the dump? The Carp River (which runs into the Ottawa River) is within one kilometre of the dump.
>
> The Ottawa River is within sight of the dump.
>
> How about the leachate pipeline under the Carp Road that empties directly into the City sewer at the corner of Hazeldean and Carp Road? The leachate is then dumped into the Ottawa River at Greens Creek.
>
> This should be enough information to get you excited about the proposed expansion of the dump.
>
> So far only a few groups of concerned citizens have taken action: No Dump.ca. Richardson Corridor Association and Ottawa Landfillwatch.org.

They are waiting your input to help stop this expansion. Please rise up to the challenge and act before it is too late. After all, you are the "Ottawa Riverkeeper."

According to Chasles, they offered no assistance or even moral support, so a few days later, on April 12, Chasles sent another email to the Riverkeeper pointing out that Waste Management had admitted that untreated leachate from the Carp Road dump goes directly into the City of Ottawa sewers and then into the Ottawa River. The sewage treatment plant through which it passes is designed only for human waste and does not remove harmful chemicals according to Chasles.

Still no assistance from the Riverkeeper, or any environmental group. A 1,100-page brief to City Council presented in late May was compiled entirely by volunteers from Stittsville and it is they and they alone who continue the battle against the expansion. Similar situations have occurred at several other communities across Ontario, including Sarnia and Napanee.

There is no doubt the Sierra Club and most other environmental groups, along with the NDP and most Liberals, advocate much greater diversion (recycling) of garbage, which is a noble endeavour, but anyone who believes that we will ever be able to recycle all of the garbage we produce or anything approaching 90 percent is living in a dream world. And even if we did achieve that lofty goal, the question of what we do with existing landfill sites (garbage dumps) still remains. All the dreaming and recycling in the world isn't going to make the Carp Mountain disappear!

• • •

What I find very strange and more than a little sad is that the environmental movement, including the Sierra Club, the Ottawa Riverkeeper, and Friends of the Carp River, won't get behind and actively promote a practical solution for waste disposal other that recycling.

What's even worse, the Sierra Club seems to be actively supporting dumps like the Carp Mountain. On May 21, 2006, even as local residents were presenting their 1,100-page brief at Ottawa City Hall, calling on council to find new innovative methods of waste disposal, including incineration, representatives from the Sierra Club were passing out brochures claiming that if we just did it their way we could reduce our garbage by as much as 90 or 95 percent, something no country or municipality on earth has ever been able to do or even close! Several of the community representatives, all volunteers, tell me they were devastated by this attempt to destroy all their hard work.

Why would anyone, let alone an organization claiming to champion the environment, do something like that? These organizations must be fully aware that dangerous chemicals leaking from these dumps are a danger to our soil, the ground water, and our lakes, rivers, and streams.

Good heavens, former NDP MPP and now extreme left-wing Ottawa City Councillor Alex Cullen, during the height of the Carp Mountain controversy, issued a warning to Ottawa taxpayers not to throw any of these newfangled low-energy light bulbs into the garbage, because according to Cullen, "they contain mercury which might leak out of the dumpsites and create serious health problems!"

When I confronted Mr. Cullen on this and asked him if he was admitting then that the dumpsites were leaking dangerous toxins that could threaten the public's health, he would only repeat that mercury from the new low-energy light bulbs might pose a public health hazard if they were sent to a dumpsite.

I found it more than passing strange that he and several other members of council didn't seem concerned about millions of tons of heaven only knows what dangerous toxic material that has already been dumped into landfill sites across the province, but are warning us about minute quantities of mercury in light bulbs! I tried to point out to Mr. Cullen and others that if mercury from light bulbs is believed to be hazardous to our health, then surely it means the dumps are leaking and the authorities know it but couldn't care less. Go figure!

TWENTY

Some Solutions

It's not as though there aren't all kinds of very viable examples of modern, pollution-free waste disposal methods. In Ontario, for example, there is a high-efficiency incinerator burning about 30 percent of all the garbage produced by the more than one million residents of Peel Region (the Brampton area). And by the way, Peel has just opened a new state-of-the-art single-stream recycling facility. This is a system whereby residents don't have to sort their garbage. None of this business about putting some stuff in a blue box, some in a green box, and so on. In Peel, you put your garbage out like we used to—in green garbage bags—and all the sorting is done at the recycling facility. Common sense dictates that will greatly increase the level of recycling. In fact, Peel estimates that within two or three years, all their garbage will either be recycled or burned in their high-efficiency incinerator.

Sweden may have the best solution of all.

According to Magnus Schonning, First Secretary of the Swedish Embassy in Ottawa, we need a four-pronged approach. Reduce the amount of packaging through tax incentives, recycle as much as possible, recover energy from biological waste (compost), and burn the rest in high-efficiency incinerators to produce electricity.

"For instance," says Schonning, "in Sweden you won't find toothpaste tubes packaged in boxes. The tax structure encourages manufacturers to improve production methods and reduce packaging."

The second step encourages citizens to recycle, although in this area the Swedes could learn a lesson from Peel. The Swedish recycling rate is only 33 percent, quite likely because their system requires residents to separate waste into different bins. Peel's single-stream recycling facility, which expects to recycle as much as 60 percent of all waste, would obviously be an improvement on that.

The third step in Sweden is a form of rapid composting of biological waste. About 10 percent of their waste is composted to produce biogas, fertilizer, and soil.

The fourth step is high-efficiency incineration. In fact, fully 47 percent of all of Sweden's waste is now burned in 29 energy-producing incinerators.

The largest of these is the Savenas incinerator located outside Gothenburg, which burns 460,000 tons of waste per year. Schonning says it would cost Ottawa $286 million to build a similar facility at the Carp Road landfill site and $29 million to maintain and operate the facility each year. According to him, using the Savenas plant as a guide, the energy produced by such an incinerator would generate $30 to $70 million in energy sales each year and the investment would pay off in four to ten years.

Schonning says the increase in energy production from

waste lowers Sweden's dependency on fossil fuels, reducing carbon dioxide emissions and helping that country to fulfill its Kyoto commitments. The leftover bottom ash can be used to build roads and the excess fly ash can be stored in landfills perfectly safely.

Any time I have raised the issue of incineration with so-called environmentalists, the issue of dioxins is always raised. Examine most arguments against incineration and almost invariably you will see claims that they produce dangerous dioxins. Therefore, it is important to pay close attention to what Schonning has to say next:

"Dioxins are no longer an issue with high-efficiency incineration." According to Schonning: "Sweden's annual emissions from incinerators produce *less than one gram* of dioxin per year, compared to the 5 to 30 grams of dioxins produced by landfill site fires. Non-controlled landfill fires are a much bigger problem than controlled combustion in incinerators."

Schonning says it is sad to follow the debate about incinerators in Canada. "Here," he says, "incineration is seen as hazardous to human health and the environment as a whole. In Sweden, the government has set out national targets to reduce household waste going to landfills, while promoting incineration as a safe way to take care of waste and to generate heat and electricity.

"How have our two countries come to such different positions on waste management?" he asks. The answer may be that many Canadians base their opinions on outdated information. "For example," says Schonning, "[Ottawa City] councillor Peter Hume said, governments looked at incinerators in the late 1980s but they were rejected for environmental and health concerns due to toxic emissions.

"It's true that in the 1980s incinerators had problems with the emissions of toxic substances. However, in Sweden, modern technology has reduced these emissions drastically with a 90 to 99 percent decrease in emissions of mercury, lead, cadmium, and zinc during the years 1985 to 2004."

Sharon Labchuk, the Green Party's environmental critic expresses very legitimate concerns about dioxins. Unfortunately, she too is getting her facts from outdated sources. Fifteen years ago, all 18 Swedish waste-incineration plants emitted about 100 grams of dioxins per year. Today dioxin emissions from the 29 Swedish waste-incineration plants amount to a total of 0.7 grams.

The Dutch Government has outlawed dumping any waste that can be burned, although it is estimated that some 1.4 million tons still ends up in landfill sites because of a lack of incineration capacity. More incineration plants are under construction at several sites across the country.

One of the largest incinerators is at Alkmaar that burns about 470,000 tons per year of household and industrial waste produced by the area's 1.4 million residents. This plant, along with all others in Holland, produces electricity and heat with the bottom ash being used as a filler in asphalt and as a substitute for lime and marl. The Dutch Government monitors all incinerators closely and, in line with the Swedish experience, has reduced dioxins to almost nothing.

If you would like further information on the Dutch experience, check out this website: www.minvrom.nl.

With all the evidence now before us, it begs this question. Why in the world are most of those involved in the so-called environmental movement still opposed to any form of incineration?

And don't try giving me that old excuse that landfill sites (dumps) are much cheaper than incineration. Has anyone ever figured out what it costs to maintain a dumpsite after it is closed? We taxpayers and those who come after us will have to maintain these sites for hundreds of years. You just don't bury garbage and forget about it. Oh no! As just one example, the former March landfill site in the City of Ottawa, which is now closed, costs between $200,000 and $450,000 per year to maintain. And believe you me, the March dump is miniscule compared to the Carp Road site. All these sites will eventually need to be cleaned up and maintained forever. What do you suppose the cost of that will be?

• • •

One of the ironic aspects of the Left's battle against modern methods of garbage disposal is that on this issue they are getting into bed not only with big business, but American big business!

According to its own website, Waste Management of Canada is a giant corporation based in the United States with stated revenue in the fourth quarter of 2005 of $3.37 billion and net income for the quarter of $290 million. The company projects net cash of $2.4 billion in 2006. The company operates 289 active sites in North America, handles 115 million tons per year, and has 429 collection sites, 366 transfer stations, and some 21 million customers. In addition, Waste Management Corporation is the largest recycler in North

America with 138 recycling plants. In short, this is one mother of a company!

Which brings us to another thing that puzzles me greatly. Why are the environmentalists and giant corporations on the same side on this issue? Could it have anything to do with money?

There is no segment of the business world that stands to lose more money when we begin to utilize modern garbage disposal methods than the extremely profitable recycling industry. Please keep in mind the real money with recycling is in the additional second or even third curb pickup service which will no longer be required with the advent of mainstream recycling, incineration, or gasification.

With mainstreaming our garbage, followed by incineration at the same location, you don't need all the extra trucks, bins, boxes, and storage and recycling facilities. It's all done there at one location.

And if money is not involved in the Left's battle against modern waste disposal methods, then what is? There seems to be only one other explanation.

Think of it. If they aren't doing it for money, then the environmentalists and their friends want to create garbage mountains as nothing more than punishment for not living our lives the way most left-wing organizations and individuals think we should. Fact is, according to them, we poor benighted buggers out here in the trenches just don't understand the higher moral plane at which the social engineers operate. We need to "grow," have our "consciousness raised," "educate ourselves" and recognize the moral superiority of the Sierra Clubs of the world. We deserve the garbage until we all smarten up and get socially engineered into the wonderful new nirvana the Left is preparing for us. Until we do, mountains of stinking garbage are our just desserts!

The Left likes to call itself "progressive," but how insisting on 14th century methods of waste disposal can be considered progressive sure beats the leachate out of me!

TWENTY-ONE

The Attack on Families

In his book *The Vision of the Anointed: Self-Congratulation As a Basis for Social Policy* (Basic Books, 1996), Thomas Sowell writes:

> The family is inherently an obstacle to schemes for central control of social processes. Therefore the anointed necessarily find themselves repeatedly on a collision course with the family. It is not a matter of any subjective animus on their part against families. The anointed may in fact be willing to shower government largess upon families as they do on other social entities. But the preservation of the family as an autonomous decision-making unit is incompatible with the third-party decision making that is at the heart of the vision of the anointed.

Sowell goes on to state the manner in which the incidents of various problems in families are overstated by "artful definitions and half truths." He points to the coverage given to domestic violence that would have us believe that most wives are at great risk of being beaten by their husbands. The fact is, says Sowell, that the traditional family is the safest setting for a woman.

The rate of violence, he says, for example, among lesbians living together is about the same as heterosexual couples but you never hear of this because it doesn't suit the agenda of those who would have us believe that male-female relationships are violence prone.

If what Sowell says is true—that the family stands in the way of what he calls central control of the social system—it certainly helps to explain the Left's continuing efforts to wrest control of children from their parents.

There is no better illustration of this than the decades-old struggle by concerned parents and various conservative political and social movements to get the age of sexual consent raised from 14 to, at the very least, 16.

As I write this, the new Conservative Minister of Justice, Vic Toews, is promising to table a bill in Parliament to raise the age of sexual consent to 16. He calls it the "Age of Protection" bill. Amazingly enough, this time the NDP says it may support the bill, although in past years any attempt to raise the age of sexual consent has been fought tooth and nail by almost all in the NDP, Bloc, and Liberal benches.

I hope by the time you read this the bill has passed, but the fact it has taken this long to accomplish what any parent of teenaged children knows is right, is a stark testament to the anti-family ideology displayed by much of the Left in this country.

It's a terrible thing to think that the day after a child turns 14, they can have consensual sex with an adult of any age, and there is nothing the parents can legally do to prevent it.

Think of it! The law states that parents have a legal responsibility to ensure that their children attend school until at least the age of 16. Thus it is, I suppose, that a father must stand outside her "boyfriend's" door patiently waiting until his 14-year-old daughter finishes a bout of sex with a 25-year-old man before he can insist she get herself off to school!

And by the way, parental authority as it applies to sexual conduct, doesn't come to a screeching halt at age 14 only with our daughters. Our sons can, likewise, legally engage in anal sex with adult males the day they turn 14.

How this came about is a fascinating story with very powerful anti-family undertones.

The Criminal Code of Canada states that anal intercourse is unlawful under the age of 18 for unmarried persons, but two lower courts, the Quebec Court of Appeal and the Ontario Court of Appeal, have both declared that section of the code is unconstitutional. Despite what the Criminal Code may say, that is to say, despite what the Parliament of Canada deemed unlawful, anal intercourse, for all intents and purposes, is legal across Canada for all persons aged 14 and over. The only exceptions that apply to the legality of all forms of sexual relations deal with situations where a relationship of trust exists between the adult and child (for example, between a teacher and pupil).

• • •

It happened in 1995. A 23-year-old man was charged with several sexual offences involving his fiancée's niece. A judge ruled that while the girl was only 13 when vaginal sex began, the anal intercourse only started when she was 14 and was consensual.

The man was convicted on several charges of sexual interference with a minor under the age of 14 but was acquitted on the charge of anal intercourse by the judge who ruled that, although the law prohibits anal intercourse until the age of 18, the law is unconstitutional because it denies the accused the defence of consent.

The Crown appealed this decision and was opposed by (believe it or not) the Canadian Foundation for Children, Youth and the Law. The Foundation argued that outlawing consensual anal intercourse by those under the age of 18 discriminated against young people, especially gay teens.

The Foundation, by the way, made this argument only weeks after appearing before a court in an effort to strike down section 43 of the Criminal Code, which permits spanking under some conditions. While the Foundation was unsuccessful in outlawing parental spanking, it had better luck with anal intercourse.

Madame Justice Rosalie Abella of the Ontario Court of Appeal ruled that the law dealing with anal intercourse "arbitrarily disadvantaged gay men by denying to them until the age of 18 a choice available at the age of 14 to those who are not gay, namely their choice of sexual expression with a consenting partner to whom they are not married." [Library of Parliament report, "Canada's Legal Age of Consent to Sexual Activity, prepared by Marilyn Pilon, Law and Government Division; direct reference: RvM © 1995, 23 O.P., 3d 629.]

Today Rosalie Abella is a member of the Supreme Court of Canada.

There are so many incongruities in all of this it is hard to know what is the most outrageous, but it's mighty difficult to top an organization purporting to work on behalf of children, working to destroy parental authority, not once but twice in the same month! Imagine! Lobbying government to make criminals of parents who spank their children, then in the next breath demanding that it be legal for a 45-year-old man to have anal sex with your 14-year-old son, or daughter!

Through all of this, most Liberals, the NDP and the Bloc have steadfastly refused to raise the age of sexual consent. Time after time various organizations including Citizens Against Child Exploitation, the Canadian Association of Chiefs of Police, and Conservative MPs have demanded that the age of sexual consent be raised to 16 or even 18. All to no avail.

Some minor changes have been made to the legislation but to quote the Library of Canada's Parliamentary Information and Research Service, "The Criminal Code does not now criminalize consensual sexual activity with or between persons 14 or over, unless it takes places in a relationship of trust or dependency, in which case sexual activity with persons over 14 but under 18 can constitute an offence notwithstanding their consent. Even consensual activity with those under 14 but over 12 may not be an offence if the accused is under 16 and less than two years older than the complainant."

If and when the Conservatives new "Age of Protection" bill is passed it will include clauses allowing some sexual relations between children of approximately the same age. (The proposal, as I write this, is that an age difference of five years maximum would be legal.)

As Vic Toews says, "We have no intention of making criminals out of children experimenting with sex, but we must do something to prevent the exploitation of children by adults, especially in this new age of the Internet."

The Left has fought raising the age of sexual consent for decades and some will continue to fight since extending parental authority in any way obviously doesn't suit their agenda. These, after all, are the same people who want to send our just barely toddlers out to state-run daycare institutions, and have fought tooth and nail against any kind of tax or other incentives to encourage or assist stay-at-home parents.

Those who continue to fight for the right of our children to have sex with adults and discourage stay-at-home parenting may claim they are not anti-family, but remember that embarrassing statement that came out of the Liberal camp about parents spending money on beer and popcorn rather than on their children? It may be far more revealing than most of us suspect!

And if you wish to argue that government policy up until this point has not been intended to discourage family life, you will have to explain why our tax system penalizes families where a parent stays home with their children. Taxing individuals rather than families places the parent-in-the-home family at a considerable financial disadvantage. Most countries make a much greater effort to support families than we do in Canada. In the United States, for example, not only is the tax rate on average about 20 percent below that in this country, but all the interest paid on a home mortgage is tax deductible. Since many young couples decide to have children only after they can afford a house, this is a terrific boost for families.

Even other socialist countries seem much more interested in the promotion of family life than we here in Canada. France, for example, has a very unique tax system highly supportive of families. In that country the incomes of all family members, including children living in the home, are combined and classed as one family's income. This then can be split among all family members, whether they are earning income or not. Children are weighted only half as much as their parents. In other words, suppose the entire family-of-four income (in Canadian dollars) is $102,000, all earned by one person. The mother and father would each be allowed to declare an income of $34,000, each child $17,000.

If you were to transpose that income-splitting situation to Canada, the tax savings for the one-income-earner family would be close to half!

Finland is also extremely pro-family. There, various forms of financial incentives are available that allow a parent to remain in the home with a child for the first three years, or if they choose, they can place the child in readily available government-run daycare. Guess what? In Finland, 72 percent of parents choose to take the childcare allowance for one of them to remain in the home for the first three years of the child's life. In Finland, where parents have a choice, only 11 percent choose state-run daycare.

There are studies and surveys that indicate that if Canada were truly family friendly and offered similar incentives for a parent to stay at home during those early years, the overwhelming majority of families would do exactly that.

What is very revealing is that in many cases the same people opposed to raising the age of sexual consent are the same ones who discourage stay-at-home parents.

Why is that?

TWENTY-TWO

Six Singhs

It's 1985. Six men from India, all with the surname Singh, show up at the Supreme Court of Canada to appeal a deportation order issued by the Immigration Appeal Board, and all hell breaks loose!

The six Singhs claim they will be persecuted in India if forced to return because of their association with the Akali Dal political party in the Punjab.

They hit pay dirt! On the Court is outspoken and far left-wing judge Bertha Wilson, who has what can only be called a very "liberal" interpretation of the Charter of Rights and Freedoms. She writes a ruling that throws Canada's refugee system into total chaos, creating a foolhardy and very dangerous mess that plagues us to this day.

Judge Wilson rules that the refugee system as it exists in 1985 violates the Charter, which she says guarantees everyone on Canadian soil, including asylum seekers, the right to fundamental justice.

Two of the sitting justices agree with her. Three others are silent on a refugee claimant's Charter rights, but rule that the

Immigration Appeal Board violates a claimant's right to an oral hearing as protected in the Bill of Rights.

In practical terms what the ruling means is that anyone— no matter the reason, no matter how undesirable that person may be—must be granted all the rights and freedoms (except voting rights) afforded Canadian citizens under the Charter.

Set one foot on Canadian soil, declare refugee status, and with any luck and a good immigration lawyer you're in for good! Even if years later they get around to ordering you deported, any self-respecting claimant can use the appeal system (at our expense) and stall for years until a court rules that you've been here so long it would be cruel to boot you out. Having a couple of kids on Canadian soil also works very well. So does marrying a Canadian.

As you can imagine, this news spreads like wildfire throughout the messed-up part of the world from which many people are prepared to pay large sums of money to escape. By the time our government gets around to dealing with Judge Wilson's new ruling and creates the Refugee Appeal Board it's four years later, 1989, and a staggering 115,000 people, all claiming refugee status, have descended on us like a giant swarm of locusts anxious for manna, not from heaven, but rather courtesy of the long-suffering Canadian taxpayer!

In the early years after the "Singh" decision, anyone who showed up at our border and claimed refugee status could be almost certain they would be admitted to Canada, and provided free legal assistance, welfare, education, health care, and accommodation, no questions asked.

We will probably never know exactly how many were simply "waved through" the immigration process without even checking to see if the names provided were accurate. Tens of thousands, to be sure.

And even if the board did actually hear the claim, entry was almost guaranteed anyway. Of the 12,000 claimants who appeared before the board in 1989, almost 90 percent were allowed in.

It's obvious not much, if anything, has changed. Recently, the deputy director of operations of Canada's "spy agency," CSIS, Jack Hooper, tells a shocked Senate committee that only about 10 percent of immigrants and refugees arriving from such terrorist hotbeds as Pakistan and Afghanistan receive any security screening.

We may as well post signs along the roadways and back alleys of every Third World and war-torn nation on earth saying "Canada welcomes your scoundrels, your warlords, your terrorists, your killers, torturers, and rapists. Free lawyers, free room and board, free health and dental care, free education, free eye glasses...

We have tightened up our borders a bit since 9/11. They tell us that last year only 40 percent of the refugee applications were accepted, but that really doesn't mean much. Because even in those rare instances where a refugee appeal is turned down it is virtually impossible to actually send the applicants back to the country from which they came.

Have a look at the appeal process and you'll understand why. Here are the steps failed claimants may take:

1. Seek judicial review in the Federal Court, which only considers mistakes in law. The success rate here is only about 10 percent.

2. Request a pre-removal risk assessment that examines

whether rejected refugees would face torture or danger if deported. The success rate here is very low, only about 4 percent.

3. File a humanitarian and compassionate review, arguing they would suffer unusual hardship if removed. Here the success rate is better than 60 percent.

4. Then if all the three previous appeals are turned down you can ask the Federal Court to review the negative decisions in the three other appeals.

• • •

This process can and often does last for years and costs taxpayers tens of millions of dollars. In Ontario, for example, in 2004, some 14,000 refugee claimants collected $115 million in welfare alone. During the same year, the legal aid costs for refugee claimants in Ontario exceeded $16 million.

Another very disturbing aspect of our refugee system is that, by and large, real refugees simply don't have the resources to make it to Canada. For the most part, refugees who arrive at our borders are those who can afford either a real or forged passport, as well as a return airline ticket from the country of origin.

Today you cannot board an aircraft for international travel to most countries without a passport as well as a return airline ticket. As an indication of how accurate that statement is, consider the fact that last year democratic countries such as India, Mexico, and Costa Rica were among the top ten source countries while war-torn nations such as Rwanda, Sudan, and Afghanistan were nowhere near the top of the list.

One of those who has expressed grave concern over the

state of Canada's refugee system is former Deputy Prime Minister John Manley who says, "There is no shortage of refugees in the world and we can meet our obligations by bringing people largely from United Nations Refugee Camps anywhere in the world. These are genuine people who have fled for fear of losing their lives... People who get to Canada because they've got the money and connections shouldn't be at the top of our list."

Unfortunately, Mr. Manley and his Liberal government did almost nothing in their some 13 years of power to fix this problem. The few minor changes, such as introducing visa requirements for 12 new countries and requiring refugees who land first in the United States to seek a safe haven there rather than coming immediately to Canada, have done little to stop the influx of refugee claimants who apparently have money and connections.

And, in particular, nothing has been done to ensure that those ordered deported actually leave the country.

In 2003, Auditor General Sheila Fraser was highly critical of our immigration enforcement system. She referred to incomplete computer databases, a lack of detention spaces, long drawn-out court battles often lasting years, and a so-called removal pipeline that was incredibly clogged.

Ms. Fraser found that there were 11,000 cases of refugees already in Canada who hadn't even been assigned to anyone for assessment! Even worse, she found that some 30,000 refugees had outstanding arrest warrants for removal that had never been enforced. Some had been ordered deported seven years previously, but the warrants never served. Add to that figure the 11,000 individuals wandering about like some lost Biblical tribe in a Canadian desert of incompetence and confusion and you have at least 40,000 people from some of the most corrupt and violent countries in the world doing heaven only knows what in this country!

The RCMP recently announced that they believe at least three thousand of the "missing" are known criminals. Just to ensure that none of these are caught, our civil libertarians insist that neither the pictures nor descriptions of those being sought can be released to the public. Yes! That's right, today at least 40,000 foreign nationals ordered deported have gone "missing" and out of our concern for their privacy and civil rights we are not allowed to know their names, or descriptions! And you still don't think the Left has gone nuts?!

TWENTY-THREE

The Amazing Mr. Mohammad

On April 27, 1999 the Canadian Jewish Congress (CJC) issued the following press release:

> "All Canadians who abhor the scourge of terrorism will welcome the recent issuance of a new deportation order against convicted terrorist Mahmoud Mohammad Issa Mohammad," stated Canadian Jewish Congress President Moshe Ronen.
>
> Mr. Ronen noted that "People everywhere bear the many scars which terrorism has inflicted. Canada itself has not been immune because terrorism does not discriminate as to its targets and it knows no boundaries. If the international community is to be successful in eradicating terrorism there can be no moratorium on terrorists. By staying the course in regards to Mahmoud Mohammad, Canada has affirmed that terrorism will not be tolerated."
>
> In addition, CJC is pleased that after so many years, the attempt by Mahmoud Mohammad to avoid deportation by claiming refugee status has finally ground to a halt. Stated Mr. Ronen, "Accepting such a claim from a convicted terrorist who lied upon entering Canada would have made a mockery of our refugee determination system. Such flagrant abuse would tarnish Canada's reputation as a country prepared to do its share to fight terrorism while welcoming genuine asylum seekers whose lives are at risk."

Brave, noble words from an obviously thankful Canadian Jewish Congress.

There's just one hitch: It's now almost eight years later and

Mahmoud Mohammad Issa Mohammad is still living comfortably in Brantford, Ontario. That final deportation order wasn't final!

The amazing Mr. Mohammad began his career as a gunman with the Popular Front for the Liberation of Palestine (PFLP). In 1968, Mohammad and an accomplice hijacked an El Al jetliner at the Athens Airport, threw a grenade at the plane, and raked it with machine-gun fire, killing one passenger.

Mohammad was caught by Greek police, convicted, and sentenced to 17 years in prison. Less than two years later, in 1970, six Palestinian terrorists hijacked a Greek airliner, once again in Athens, and threatened to kill all the passengers if Mohammad wasn't released. Greek authorities caved in and released Mohammad, who somehow escaped to Cyprus and then Spain, and finally very mysteriously, on February 25, 1987, he showed up at a Canadian border point with his wife Fadia and two children and, even more mysteriously, was given landed immigrant status!

The claim from immigration authorities is that he forgot to mention that he was a wanted criminal and apparently also forgot to tell authorities his real name.

In fairly typical fashion, it took the government about a year to discover who Mohammad really was, and in December of 1988 a deportation order was issued. The first of many!

Some 18 years and countless court battles later, the truly amazing Mr. Mohammad is still here, a symbol, if ever there was one, of what is wrong with our immigration and refugee system. But by no means is this the only smouldering pant load that Judge Wilson and her fellow lefties have dropped on our doorstep.

TWENTY-FOUR

The Man With a Bucket

It's doubtful that Home Depot ever intended one of their buckets to be used to cart around a severed head, but Mihaly Illes thought it was perfect for the job! "Have a look at this!" Mihaly would say, thrusting the bucket beneath a friend's nose, then popping the lid off to reveal the bullet-riddled head he was proudly carting about.

Needless to say, the Presbyterian Church of Canada, which sponsored him as a refugee from Hungary in 1992, was not amused. No sooner had Mr. Illes landed in Canada than he hooked up with a band of Eastern European mobsters and a local motorcycle gang. Clearly, he was no choirboy.

When arrested, police found him with a rifle, a semi-automatic pistol, and several other guns. He was sentenced to seven years in jail for drug dealing and in 1998 was ordered deported. Mr. Illes clearly found this to be unacceptable and during his deportation hearing stormed out of the room claiming the procedure was "a violation of my rights!"

Despite his criminal record and the fact he had threatened to kill a police officer, Mr. Illes managed to stall his deportation until the fall of 2000 when he was actually kicked out of the country. It was all a waste of time, because in a matter of months Mr. Illes was back in Canada, having passed through our porous borders as easily as you know what through a goose!

We were a little luckier this time. He'd only been dealing drugs and committing a few other crimes for about a year when police stumbled across him crossing the US border.

Investigation turned up a few of his friends who had been treated to the "head viewing." Turns out Mr. Illes had killed one of his nearest and dearest friends—28-year-old Javan Dowling, the man whose head fit so comfortably into that Home Depot bucket.

Mr. Illes was sentenced to life in prison a couple of years ago so we're stuck with not only all the expense of his first trial (his deportation), and then his second trial, but the cost of keeping him behind bars as well! We certainly did Hungary a big favour when we accepted this guy. Once again it's another example of how careless we are in accepting refugees—how sieve-like our borders are, and how well many of these people can work our "tolerant" system.

Here's another tragic story: In 1994, Clinton Junior Gayle, who had been ordered deported back to Jamaica not once but *twice* previously, was allowed to stay in Canada long enough to shoot and kill Toronto Police Constable Todd Bayliss and seriously wound Constable Mike Leone.

And then there's the famous pizza case…

TWENTY-FIVE

Double Cheese, Please, and Hold the Olives

There must be a lot of money in pizza. There certainly seems to have been for Harjit Singh who, from all reports, ran a dandy little pizza parlour up until recently in Brampton. Up until February 5, 2005, to be precise, when at the government's insistence and assistance, he boarded a plane for India. As always with a deportation order, he had only a one-way ticket.

There was probably no one happier to see him shut down his ovens than Judy Sgro, the woman who had been Minister of Immigration only three weeks earlier. Remember Judy?

That's right! Harjit Singh is the guy who claimed that Ms. Sgro had promised to help him in his attempts to avoid deportation in return for him supplying free pizzas, garlic bread, and 15 or 16 volunteers to her election headquarters during the run-up to the June 28, 2004, federal election. Ms Sgro resigned as Minister on January 14, 2005, in order, she said, to properly fight the "false allegations."

She subsequently launched a $750,000 lawsuit against Singh, so we'll let the courts decide the issue of free pizza and garlic bread. Much more revealing is the story of how Harjit Singh, was able to remain in Canada for 13 years after being ordered deported.

Harjit Singh applied for refugee status in Canada in 1988 after having been convicted of migrant smuggling in India. Some four years later, in 1992, his application was rejected and he was ordered deported.

As usual, it meant absolutely nothing. Despite having charges of people-smuggling in Canada dropped, after claims that he threatened witnesses, and then being found civilly liable in a million-dollar credit card fraud, he managed to evade deportation by filing no fewer than six appeals on humanitarian grounds, followed by numerous appeals to the Federal Court, claiming if he returned to India he would be tortured.

Singh carried out this lovely little dance, much of it at tax-payer expense, for 13 years until finally, after bringing down a cabinet minister, he was hustled aboard that plane bound for India. He was in tears as he waited in Pearson International Airport. "I'm scared," he told reporters. "I'm afraid to go back. I don't know what will happen to me."

Well, guess what? For 13 years he was able to convince the bleeding hearts on the various appeal boards and courts that he faced grave danger if deported to India. The only people who obviously didn't know anything about this were the Indian authorities, because according to an article entitled "Broken Gates" that appeared in the *Globe & Mail* on April 16, 2005, written by Marina Jimenez, Harjit Singh is now busily finishing up a new $300,000 pale pink home complete with a new bright red motorcycle parked in the driveway in an upscale district of Jalandhar! No signs of torture anywhere!

As the *Globe & Mail* says, if he ever tires of his life as a well-heeled landowner in India and returns to Canada it would be fairly easy. All he would have to do is put his finely honed skills to work and slip in under a false identity. If immigration in Canada failed to detect the falsehood, he would not be finger-printed. Unless he committed another crime and got caught, nobody would ever know that Harjit Singh was back!

And please keep in mind that shortly after 9/11, Citizenship and Immigration Minister Elinor Caplan responded to concerns about Canada's immigration and refugee system by stating: "Our laws are amongst the toughest in the world when it comes to inadmissibility for criminality and terrorism." It was also Ms. Caplan who said that any criticism concerning our immigration system or border security came from people who were "anti-immigrant, anti-everything!"

Well, there must be a lot of Canadians who are anti-immigrant, anti-everything because in the late fall of 2004, Ipsos Reid canvassed Canadians across the country asking if our refugee system requires a major rethink or adjustment. Only 26 percent replied that they thought the system was working well. Fully 71 percent demanded a major overhaul. And in response to another question, 80 percent said they believed Ottawa should be looking for ways to reduce the costs of the refugee system. Only 20 percent disagreed.

Fact is, I could fill an entire book with horror stories of heinous crimes committed by criminals who had been ordered deported but were left to wander the country freely, or were booted out of the country only to sneak back in.

At one point, Toronto police reported no fewer than four very dangerous criminals walking the streets of their city more than a year after being ordered deported. One of those was Frank Uriah Pinnock who was sentenced to six years in jail for the brutal rape of a 17-year-old girl he abducted from a bus stop. Police were outraged to find him sitting at an outdoor café in downtown Toronto one sunny day—more than a year after being ordered deported. No one had bothered to actually remove him. When police complained bitterly, he was finally sent back to Jamaica. Less than six months later, he was back in Toronto, and wanted for other serious crimes.

It is astonishing to think that even today when a dangerous criminal is ordered deported he is very often released rather than being held in custody until boarding the plane. You can be sure a good many of those 40,000 plus "missing" deportees are probably sunning themselves in some outdoor café right now, or socking back a few cold ones in your favourite neighbourhood bar. That is, if they aren't busy plotting or committing their next crime.

Fortunately, we can take great pride in knowing that we are not invading their privacy by publishing their pictures on a wanted poster someplace. And, of course, that we are protecting their civil rights!

Ahhhh…

TWENTY-SIX

The Failure-Is-Really-Success Gang!

Let me pose a question for all you parents. Suppose you've got a little two-year-old having difficulty with the concept of poo pooing on the po po, or as my grandchild says, "phew phewing." Try as you might to prevent it, "accidents" do occur every couple of days.

Along comes some whiz-bang expert who claims he's got an arm full of reports and surveys that prove he's got the perfect method to fix the problem. For a thousand dollars, he'll have little Johnny or Janie using the potty perfectly within a few days.

Two months later you've got twice the problem—now the "accidents" are daily. Do you continue with this revolutionary new miracle cure? Is creating twice the problem success?

Well, if you are the socialists who run things on the city councils of Montreal, Ottawa, Toronto, or Vancouver, the answer is a resounding yes! Doubling a serious problem in those cities is considered by the lefties on those city councils to be such a fantastic "success" that they're going to expand the program that created the "success" and spend a lot more money bringing it to a lot more people.

Think I'm kidding? Think again.

The four cities I have just mentioned have some form of needle exchange program (NEP) for their local druggie populations, which is intended to lessen the rate of hepatitis C (HEP C) and HIV infection. In every single case, the rate of infection has more than doubled since the inception of the NEPs, yet in all four cities the program has been hailed as a great success!

Such a success that in each case it is being expanded to include crack pipe paraphernalia, "shoot 'em up" free zones or houses and, in Vancouver, free drugs!

The most graphic illustration of how astonishingly stupid this program of assisting drug users is, has to be in Vancouver, which is now generally acknowledged as having the worst drug problem in North America while handing out more free needles than any other city on earth (more than two million last year). Imagine on a per capita basis more drug users in Vancouver than New York, Chicago, or Los Angeles!

But Ottawa is not far behind. Let's have a look at some of the facts presented to us not long ago in the Capital.

Ottawa began its so-called needle exchange program in 1991. A study done by University of Ottawa professor and researcher Lynne Leonard and presented to Ottawa City Council states that in 1992, 10.3 percent of the injection drug users attending the needle exchange program site, which had just begun, were HIV positive. This same report then states that after eight years of the NEP, the HIV positive rate among injection drug users had shot up to 23 percent. According to Ottawa's former Medical Officer of Health, Dr. Robert Cushman, the HIV positive rate among injection drug users in 2004 was 21 percent. Despite this doubling of the HIV infection rate since the NEP was introduced, the program was deemed to be a success by Ottawa City Council, which not only agreed to continue with the needle exchange program, but to begin a crack pipe distribution program, as well.

It gets worse. Lynne Leonard's report also states that between 1985 and 1988, prior to the launch of NEP, injection drug users accounted for 2 percent of those actually diagnosed with full-blown AIDS. As of 1999, seven years after NEP started, that figure had skyrocketed to an astounding 17 percent.

Similar increases in both HIV positive tests and HIV infections diagnosed have also occurred in Montreal, Vancouver, and Toronto.

In his attempts to persuade Ottawa City Council to launch a crack pipe program, Dr. Cushman was quoted as saying that the Capital's HEP C infection rate among intravenous drug users was 76 percent, once again a huge increase from the early 1990s. He claimed Ottawa's HIV and HEP C rates were second only to Vancouver.

A Canadian Press report on December 26, 2003, stated that in Vancouver it is now believed that 90 percent of intravenous drug users have HEP C and 30 percent are HIV positive.

Once again, all of this is deemed to be so successful that the programs to assist drug users in their criminal behaviour are being expanded.

It's a kind of Alice in Wonderland March Hare madness in combination with Orwellian "newspeak." Failure is success, disaster is triumph, so let's have lots more of it!

We shouldn't be surprised at the disaster created by the so-called needle exchange program, nor should we be surprised when eventually our new "crack pipe" giveaway blows up in our face as well. Heaven knows we've had plenty of warning.

The most definitive, unbiased study of NEP effectiveness ever done in North America was carried out in Montreal between 1988 and 1995. Published in the December 1997 edition of the *American Journal of Epidemiology*, it raised so many eyebrows in the United States that to this day the US Government refuses to assist in any funding for needle exchange programs.

The study was carried out by a research team led by doctors from the Centre de l'Université de Montreal (CHUM), St. Luc campus and the McGill University School of Medicine. They followed 1,599 subjects over a period of seven years.

The results were devastating for the supporters of NEP, or should have been if anyone on the Canadian side of the border was paying attention.

The study concluded that "injection drug users have a higher seroconversion rate (higher rate converting from HIV negative to HIV positive) when taking part in a needle exchange program than those who did not." While the researchers do not necessarily condemn needle exchange programs, they say, "these worrisome findings, however, raise questions as to the effectiveness of these programs as implemented within the context of prevention and care for drug users."

One of the reasons for the Montreal findings may be explained by something written by Dr. Catherine Hankins, a medical epidemiologist with the Montreal Regional Public Department, adjunct professor in the Department of Epidemiology and Biostatistics, McGill University and association director of the McGill AIDS Centre.

In an editorial she wrote for the Canadian Medical Association in 1997, Dr. Hankins said:

There is some concern that, in attracting injection drug users at highest risk, programs in large metropolitan areas may be serving to foster new social networks. Ultimately, we cannot rely on these programs alone to stem the HIV tide: They must be integrated with a wide range of additional services that emphasize treatment and rehabilitation over a punitive approach."

Dr. Hankins goes on to say:

In Montreal, needle exchange participants are more likely to have paying sexual partners, to be men who have sex with men and to have a higher HIV incidence than non-participants. Needle exchange programs clearly are attracting a higher risk clientele. These findings give rise to concern that large needle exchange programs in metropolitan centres may be bringing together people who otherwise might not meet, thereby creating new social networks and fostering the mixing that has been shown to increase HIV transmission.

• • •

As in Canada, it was politically correct to implement needle exchange programs in the early '90s in the US as the AIDS scare exploded. Thus there was great pressure on the US Government to fund local initiatives from various groups, in particular the many HIV/AIDS lobbies that were springing up around the country. The Americans were about to lift the ban on federal funding when the Montreal report landed on the desks of congressional leaders. Despite the ongoing pressure from around the country and attempts to discredit the findings of the study, the government ruled that until an unbiased independent scientific study was presented to them proving that needle exchange programs worked, all federal funding would remain on hold. To this date, no such report has ever been presented to the US Congress. In fact, the number of locally funded NEPs in the US has been on a steady decline in recent years as more and more evidence pours in that they were accomplishing nothing of value and might even be making things worse.

Interestingly enough, a research study in Vancouver done in 2003 appeared to almost mirror the findings of the Montreal study. When news of this leaked out, officials were quick to make excuses, claiming that the reason HIV infection rates appeared to be higher among those taking part in their NEP, was only because those taking part in the study were more "hard core" drug users than the general druggie population.

As usual, absolute and utter refusal to even entertain the idea that maybe what they were doing wasn't working.

You may have noticed that when I refer to the Ottawa NEP, I call it a so-called needle exchange program. I do this for a reason. When originally conceived, the idea was that a clean needle would be handed out in exchange for a used (dirty) one. This was to ensure that dirty needles were not left around for children or others to pick up. In recent years this practice has evolved so that today we often give out 25 needles at a time without picking up any used ones. Thus it is no longer a needle exchange program, but rather a needle distribution program. Not only do we pay for the needles, condoms, crack pipe paraphernalia, and a special van for door-to-door delivery service, but now we must pay crews who go into known drug injection sites and clean up as many as they can find.

By any definition, it borders on madness! Especially when you consider there are many countries in the world today that have programs that actually work to reduce not only HIV and HEP C infection rates, but drug use as well.

The best example of this comes from Denmark, Norway, and Sweden, where a very thorough study was conducted among intravenous drug users from 1980 through 1996. The findings are revealing.

Norway and Sweden long ago decided that rather than simply handing out free needles they would launch a professional and thorough program of counselling and testing. Denmark, on the other hand, took the path of least resistance and instituted a needle exchange program.

The study, carried out by the Norwegian Institute for Alcohol and Drug Research (http://www.ncbi.nlm.nih.gov/entrez/query. fcgi?CMD=search&DB=pubmed) found that:

> A comparison of HIV prevention strategies in Denmark, Norway, and Sweden suggests that a high level of HIV counselling and testing might be more effective than legal access to needles and syringes/needle exchange programs. Sweden and Norway with high levels of HIV counselling and testing have had significantly lower incidence rates of HIV among intravenous drug users than Denmark where there was legal access to needles and syringes and a lower level of HIV counselling and testing. In Sweden there was no legal access to drug injection equipment.
>
> CONCLUSION: Promotion and accessibility of HIV counselling and testing among intravenous drug users should be considered in countries where such a strategy is not adopted or has low priority.

Finally, there is one other point that I think deserves mentioning: Counselling and testing not only works, it is legal; so-called needle exchange programs don't work and are strictly illegal. Let me advance, as my final argument, Section 462.2 of the Criminal Code, which says:

> Everyone who knowingly imports into Canada, exports from Canada, manufactures, promotes or sells instruments or literature for illicit drug use is guilty of an offence and liable on summary conviction.
>
> a) for a first offence, to a fine not exceeding one hundred thousand dollars, or to imprisonment for a term not exceeding six months or both; or
> b) for a second or subsequent offence, to a fine not exceeding three hundred thousand dollars or imprisonment for a term not to exceed one year or both.

Is it too much to ask that our city councils obey the law? Apparently!

TWENTY-SEVEN

The Ghettoization of Canada

The balconies of Amsterdam are sending us a warning signal: Pay attention! Danger ahead! You take this path at your peril!

If you saw the CBC television special "The Enemy Within," you know what I mean. Multiculturalism, the supreme act of tolerance, clashes with a creed that despises tolerance and demonizes non-believers! For me the most disturbing image of the documentary was the row after row of satellite dishes peeking skyward from the balconies of apartment buildings which, according to the CBC, are inhabited mostly by Muslims.

At first blush it seems innocuous enough. I have just such a dish at home. But the Dutch say it has become a very serious impediment to Muslim integration into the mainstream culture of the Netherlands. Many Muslims, they claim, just simply will not view any news, information, or even entertainment delivered by Dutch television. Many prefer Al Jeezera or similar Arabic programs that often carry a very anti-Western bias. Whether the same situation exists with other cultural groups in The Netherlands was not made clear.

When almost all your news and entertainment comes from

Al Jeezera or websites even more virulently anti-Western, and your social life centres around a mosque where imams very often warn against integrating with the local community, you create an incredibly insular ghetto where it is almost impossible for anything of the national culture of the country in which you reside to leak through.

Anyone who believes the same thing is not happening here in Canada is dreaming in technicolour.

During nearly three weeks of fielding angry calls this past summer at the outset of the war between Israel and Hezbollah, I was shocked at the number of people who openly and vehemently supported Hezbollah, one of the world's most vicious terrorist groups. Many claimed they loved Hezbollah and would gladly fight for it. "They're freedom fighters," was a common assertion.

There were fantastic accusations that as many as three million Lebanese had been killed; that strangely blackened bodies proved Israel was using chemical weapons, deliberately targeting children. Several assured me it was the Jews and George Bush who attacked the twin towers. That's an old familiar refrain! Others maintained that Hezbollah had never attacked Israel, that the Jews wanted to kill all Arabs. Many of them made such outrageous claims that you had to wonder if we were on the same planet!

As the days went on and the calls became even more strident, the claims of Israeli carnage more and more graphic, it became very evident that these callers were not getting their information from the same sources most of the rest of us were tuned to. I asked a Lebanese friend about this.

"Where are these callers getting all these stories from?"

I asked. "Is it all coming in on the Web?" He looked at me as if I had lost my marbles.

"I'll tell you where this stuff is coming from," he said. "It's coming directly from the LBC (Lebanese Broadcasting Corporation) and that's by far the most balanced coverage we're getting in Arabic. The really vicious stuff—the real propaganda—is coming, believe it or not, directly from Al Jeezera, Egyptian TV, Syrian TV, and worst of all from Al-Manara."

Al-Manara, it turns out, is Hezbollah's own private television network, beamed to millions of Arabs in countries around the world, including Canada. Attempts have been made to jam the Al-Manara signal, but I have been assured by many that it is widely available in Canada. "I can take you to a place on Bank Street, where for a few dollars I can watch Al-Manara all day," one Ottawa caller assured me, "or Syrian TV, which is almost as bad!"

Neither of those channels is the least bit hesitant to portray the most graphic and horrific scenes of carnage, especially the bodies and body parts of dead children. Unlike Western television, which for the most part shuns the exploitation of the dead, Al-Manara and Syrian TV in particular, go to great lengths to be as graphic as possible. For their propaganda purposes, the more repugnant the scene the better.

When you consider that almost all news coverage from Lebanon during the war seen on mainstream Western channels, such as CNN, was under the direction and control of Hezbollah minders, and most of the rest of it came directly from Hezbollah, it is small wonder so many Canadians have such a warped view of events.

Satellite television and the Internet have changed the face

of immigration dramatically in this country. Up until a few years ago, immigrants chose to come to Canada to make a new and better life and left the old country behind. They may have retained some of their native customs, but for the most part they had no choice but to learn the language and customs of their adopted country as quickly as possible. Many never returned to their country of origin.

Today many immigrants bring the old country with them and have no desire or need to adapt to the Canadian culture, which sadly some immigrants consider to be a foreign culture, even after years of living here. Many have no intention of living out their lives here; their hope is to make their fortune and then return to their country of birth. They are Canadians of convenience only! They settle into ghettos that are virtual replicas of the neighbourhoods from which they came, right down to the television programs they watch, the newspapers and magazines they read, and the radio shows to which they listen.

Why bother with a foreign language and culture when you can bring your old neighbourhood with you while taking advantage of everything Canada has to offer?

Tragically, as we are beginning to learn, only too often bringing the old country to Canada means bringing a cartload of very nasty baggage—all of the old country's problems, hatreds, and feuds.

Certainly this is not true, in every case, but with multiculturalism and global communications, I am afraid, it becomes more possible and thus more prevalent every day.

How we can keep a country together in this fashion, I have no idea!

• • •

The mainstream media have only recently begun to question the wisdom of multiculturalism in Canada, but in Holland, traditionally one of the world's most broad-minded and tolerant societies, a major backlash against multiculturalism and immigration is now well underway.

Among other measures mentioned earlier in this book, Holland has deported some 26,000 immigrants who arrived illegally and requires anyone applying to emigrate from Middle Eastern countries to view a 105-minute movie depicting "normal" Dutch life. The film includes scenes of topless women at the beach and gay men kissing. The implicit message is that this is typical Dutch life in a very liberal society; if any of this offends you, don't come here! Other measures, including the banning of burkas, are being contemplated.

One wit on my show suggested that a similar film portraying typical Canadian life would be pretty well confined to beavers copulating and Don Cherry ranting, which would discourage all but the most desperate from coming here. All kidding aside, what is happening in Holland and in other countries, including Britain, Germany, France, and Spain, should fire a warning shot across our bow!

After all, ours is the only country in the world that has, as a stated government policy, the actual discouragement of assimilation or integration while promoting a multitude of cultural ghettos (more on that later). You cannot possibly imagine, for example, the Government of France telling their citizens that they would have to abandon French culture in favour of dozens of foreign cultures. And pay for the transformation!

To the barricades again! Off with their heads!

TWENTY-EIGHT

Are We a Country That Hates Itself?

Here in Canada, where multiculturalism has become a keystone of our national identity, the "self-chosen ones" assure us that this is what makes us a much nicer country than the United States. And yet, when you really stop to think about it, any country that agrees to give up its unique culture, and all that entails, in favour of some kind of assortment of other people's cultures, cannot have very much pride in itself. Did you ever stop to consider that? Some have suggested that only a country that hates itself would willingly do this. Can you think of another country that would?

Where did we ever get the idea that a whole assortment of other cultures, including some pretty questionable ones, is superior to the culture, the heritage, left to us by our multiracial pioneering forefathers? How this idea has been sold to the Canadian people will undoubtedly go down in history as one of the greatest deceits since the Trojan Horse.

And let's not be confused here.

Any time this topic comes up, those who question a state-sponsored multicultural policy are accused of racism. It's a charge that, until recently, was usually sufficient to still dissent or even open debate. But racism has nothing to do with it. In fact, an increasing number of ethnic voices are being added to the growing wave of criticism of our multicultural policy.

Keep in mind, please, that we welcome all races to Canada, always have, and I hope always will. Ours is a multiracial society. It's what we expect of immigrants after they arrive that has changed drastically in recent years. Multiracial is vastly different from multicultural.

This great nation was built by people of all races who came here from all parts of the world. But prior to multiculturalism, those who arrived were expected to integrate into the national culture, and they did so gratefully. They became Canadians in every way, adopting Canadian values of hard work, honesty, civility, tolerance, a love of community, and a sense of duty and loyalty to the country that adopted them. Most became very successful and are today shocked and disgusted at the very idea of abandoning the national values they helped to create.

One of the earliest critics of multiculturalism is best-selling author Neil Bissoondath whose two books, *Selling Illusions: The Cult of Multiculturalism in Canada* and *If You Love This Country: Fifteen Voices for a Unified Canada* (published in 1994 and 1995, respectively, by Penguin Books), gave us plenty of warning of the dangers we are only now beginning to see.

Salim Mansur, associate professor of political science at the University of Western Ontario and frequent newspaper columnist says: "However noble the idea of multiculturalism was and remains, its politics was invariably bent to suit the electoral requirements of the Liberal Party which was losing ground in Western Canada and Quebec. Moreover the inherent paradox of multiculturalism is its loosening effect on national identity by assisting the forces of fragmentation rather than binding a country already weakened by the politics of regionalism and separatism." ("Divided We Fall," *Toronto Sun*, June 24, 2006.)

Tarek Fatah, a Toronto writer and host of the Saturday night weekly CTS-TV show "The Muslim Chronicle," states in an article entitled "Hypocrisy Masquerading as Diversity" in the *National Post*, June 17, 2006:

> Today there is a need to upgrade Multiculturalism 1.0 with a new version—a version that moves beyond 'celebrating diversity' for its own sake and invests in the values that bind us as Canadians. What we need is a creed that respects difference, but celebrates only that which unites us.

Fatah goes on to talk about the tremendous sacrifices our ancestors have made over the centuries to create the kind of free and democratic society that is the envy of the world. Says Fatah:

> The West cannot squander these sacrifices by permitting the growth of enclaves that reject all that was won. Any multiculturalism that does not celebrate the separation of religion and state; that does not discredit the use of religion as an instrument of politics; that permits some men to invoke culture as pretext to walk five feet ahead of their wives; that tolerates the encasing of women in a tent-like prison made of black cloth; that allows accusations of blasphemy and apostasy as a tool to invoke fear and silence will not work.

Fatah concludes by saying: "If we do not reform multiculturalism to promote integration and civic secular society we risk creating a fragmented nation, divided into 21st century religious and racial tribes, suspicious of each other, and longing for the home we left behind."

Sadly, Tarek Fatah has become a tragic victim of his moderate views. Responding to death threats towards him and his family, in early August he resigned his post as communications director of the Muslim Canadian Conference. Old county baggage strikes again!

There are many in this country who claim we have already created the fragmented nation to which Fatah refers. Walk for blocks through parts of Toronto or Vancouver and you are unlikely to hear English *or* French being spoken.

What we have done, and continue to do, is create ethnic ghettos filled with not just first generation immigrants who cannot speak our languages, but a second and now even third generation that has neither wish nor need to assimilate. Indeed, with our multicultural policies, there is no need in practical terms that they do so, and no requirement on the part of the government of the land to which they have come!

TWENTY-NINE

What Was Trudeau Thinking?

It was Pierre Trudeau who officially dropped multiculturalism on our doorstep one morning. God knows what he thought was going to happen! In his later years, even he realized what a dreadful mistake he had made. In 1995, Trudeau admitted that one of his great disappointments was that his multicultural policies—"rather than helping different groups celebrate and integrate their particular diversities within the common universality of the Canadian experience—resulted in nothing more than ever-growing demands for financial entitlements from those groups."

You would think that with his superior intelligence, he should have known that discouraging immigration from traditional sources—countries with a history of democracy, the rule of law, and secularism—while promoting waves of immigration from countries with little if any understanding of how a Western democracy works, and then encouraging those immigrants to retain their culture was a recipe for disaster. Especially when some of the cultures we urge them to retain are the very reason their home countries are in chaos.

THIRTY

It's in the Charter!

The first official reference to multiculturalism appears in the report of the Bilingualism and Biculturalism Commission back in Lester Pearson's days. The commissioners who toured Canada to hear opinions on bilingualism and biculturalism were getting an earful from those of non-British, non-French origin who for the most part accepted bilingualism but rejected biculturalism.

The report found that many of these people considered Canada to be a country fundamentally multicultural, but it must be noted that the final B and B report, while mentioning the multicultural nature of Canada, clearly intended that incoming minorities should be integrated into the bicultural nature of the country. In fact, the commissioners at one point talk about immigrant groups continuing to flourish and benefit through their integration with one of the two dominant societies in Canada.

The commissioners were so insistent about minorities integrating into mainstream Canadian society that they ended Book IV of the report by concluding that in a multi-ethnic society such as Canada's, only an ongoing process of integration "can ensure respect for both the spirit of democracy and the most deep-seated human values and can engender healthy diversity within a harmonious and dynamic whole."

Sadly, nowhere in their reports did the commissioners acknowledge the need to continue to develop a unifying Canadian culture.

John Porter, a leading Canadian sociologist, published a book in 1965 (*Vertical Mosaic: An Analysis of Social Class and Power in Canada*, University of Toronto Press) that popularized the idea of creating what he called a "vertical mosaic" [of diverse ethnic, language, religious, and regional groupings] rather than the American version of the melting pot. It appealed to the anti-American sentiment that has always been bubbling just beneath the surface in Canada, and that could almost be described as one of the distinguishing features of Canadian culture.

Nonetheless, the Bicultural and Bilingual Act was made law in Canada in 1969. This stirred up a good deal of resentment among immigrant groups across the country, so only two years later, in 1971, the federal government proclaimed a policy of multiculturalism. Biculturalism was abandoned as a national policy.

Slightly more than a year later, in 1973, a Canadian Consultative Council of Multiculturalism was formed, as well as a Multiculturalism Directorate within the Department of the Secretary of State. The great march towards official multiculturalism was launched. So much so, that in 1982 multiculturalism was entrenched in the Canadian Charter of Rights and Freedoms. Section 27 of the Charter states: "This Charter shall be interpreted in a manner consistent with the preservation and enhancement of the multicultural heritage of Canadians." In other words, the ability of an immigrant to retain his or her own native culture isn't simply a privilege in Canada. It is a right protected under the Charter.

When an Ottawa lawyer recently suggested that police hadn't taken the accused's foreign culture into account when laying charges of raping his seven-year-old daughter and rubbing chili peppers into the eyes of his other children, many observers were outraged. Whether the judge took cultural differences into account when acquitting the father of all charges, we will never know, but close examination of the Charter suggests that the courts must take Canada's multicultural "reality" into account when making decisions.

By the time Brian Mulroney came along in 1984, most Canadians had become convinced that we were the world's only full-fledged multicultural nation and, as a consequence, were a much kinder, gentler, more tolerant, lovable people than any other. Above all else, we were told it made us much better than those damn Americans and their melting pot!

Thus there was little or no questioning of a decision to confirm the principle of multiculturalism in law, and the "Act for the Preservation and Enhancement of Multiculturalism in Canada" was passed in Parliament on July 7, 1988. This made Canada the first country in the world to pass a national multiculturalism law. The Act acknowledged multiculturalism as a fundamental characteristic of Canadian society with an integral role in the decision-making process of the federal government. It stated that the policy of the Government of Canada was now to "promote multiculturalism defined as the protection and retention of incoming cultures and their languages."

The Multiculturalism Act was followed in 1991 by the Department of Multiculturalism and Citizenship Act spelling out the Minister's responsibility in encouraging the awareness of our multicultural nature. There is nothing in this act that addresses the issue of promoting national unity or building a distinctively Canadian culture. Rather, it is riddled with references to cultural retention of ethnic minorities. In effect, the Act specifically discourages the creation of a distinctive Canadian identity or culture. Astonishing!

If you would like further evidence of this dangerous folly, read a paper prepared by Marc Leman of the Political and Social Affairs Division of the Library of Parliament and available on-line at http://www.parl.gc.ca/information/library/PRBpubs/936-e.htm. Let me quote the second paragraph:

> As fact, "multiculturalism" in Canada refers to the presence and persistence of diverse racial and ethnic minorities who define themselves as different and who wish to remain so. Ideologically, multiculturalism consists of a relatively coherent set of ideas and ideals pertaining to the celebration of Canada's cultural mosaic. Multiculturalism at the policy level is structured around the management of diversity through formal initiatives in the federal, provincial and municipal domains. Finally, multiculturalism is the process by which racial and ethnic minorities compete with central authorities for achievement of certain goals and aspirations.

Lovely isn't it? Anyone who reads that would have to conclude that what the federal government of Canada is doing is creating a whole set of separate little nations based on race, religion, and ethnicity. All of these little diverse nations compete with elected governments. And not a word about integration, joining the mainstream Canadian life, or promoting a distinct Canadian culture; nothing about encouraging national unity, only a celebration of our diversity—that which divides us!

That, don't forget, is official government policy. It's bad

enough we taxpayers get stuck with paying for separatist MPs and bureaucrats, who work to destroy Canada, we've also got to pay for various racial and ethnic groups to stay separate from mainstream Canadian life!

You could not possibly find a better way to destroy the European, Judeo-Christian nature of the country our ancestors built for us and replace it with a balkanized Third World of feuding tribes and religions. Is this what Trudeau intended? Did he really believe that Canada was a nation without a culture? That we are only some kind of basket into which can be fitted a few dozen foreign cultures, each going their separate way? And what about those great statesmen in both the Conservative and Liberal parties who have carried the torch for this for more than 40 years? Was the caller to my show correct that day in June when he angrily informed me that even though he had been in Canada for 20 years, he was sending his children to an Arabic school in Toronto because, as he spat out, "Canada doesn't have a culture"? And if that caller, after 20 years in this country, has nothing but contempt for us, how do recent arrivals feel?

While you cannot blame multicultural policies for all Islamist terrorism that threatens to tear the world apart, what they learned in Britain, and we are beginning to learn in Canada, is that far from providing protection from terrorism, multiculturalism provides a fertile breeding ground for it.

Think of it. In Canada, the Charter protects multiculturalism. This means that under the law all minority cultures must be given equal status with the majority. Further to that, any attempt to impose the majority culture on the minorities is racist and illegal.

How then does the majority culture protect itself? Can we legally insist that incoming cultures integrate in any fashion? If we wanted to insist that religious symbols be banned from public schools, as they have done in France, could we? If we decided that burkas should not be worn in public, would we have the legal right to make it so? It is doubtful. In fact, there is growing speculation that despite the wishes of the Ontario Government, the banning of sharia law would not stand a Charter challenge.

How can a nation avoid chaos when the law of the land dictates that there can be no all-encompassing dominant culture? No framework of shared values; no common thread of understanding of history or heritage; no common agreement about the responsibilities without which a nation will plunge into the kind of chaos that prompted many to seek our shores in the first place.

Surely if all cultures—no matter how some may repel the majority—have equal status, then what we have created is a cultural Tower of Babel.

Exacerbating the problem in Canada is this business of dual citizenship. Canadians of all political stripes were flabbergasted during the first days of the most recent war in Lebanon to discover that there may be as many as 30,000 to 40,000 people living permanently in Lebanon but holding Canadian passports. Some of these Canadians demanding immediate evacuation hadn't lived in or paid taxes in Canada for 15 or 20 years. We are told there may be as many as 100,000 permanent residents of Hong Kong and Macao who can claim to be Canadian citizens. In Britain, they call these people "bolt-hole citizens"—people who hold two or more citizenships as a safe hole to which they can bolt in times of trouble! Best-selling author Yann Martel (*The Life of Pi*) says Canada has become the world's number-one hotel!

If we keep going the way we are, one day we may awake to find that hardly anyone calls this their country anymore, except, of course, when things get a little dicey back home!

Lovely, just bloody lovely… What a way to build a country!

THIRTY-ONE

Who Benefits?

Immediately following the deadly suicide bombings in London in July 2005, a survey throughout Britain revealed a startling fact: An estimated 26 percent of the country's 1.6 million Muslims felt no loyalty to Britain. Three thousand had received some training in al Qaeda camps and as many as 16,000 were actively engaged in or supported terrorist activity.

Canada has about half as many Muslims. If our figures in any way resemble those of Britain, we can assume that close to 200,000 Canadian Muslims feel no loyalty to this country, some 1,500 have had training in an al Qaeda camp and some 8,000 are actively engaged in or support terrorist activity.

Some will question those figures, I am sure, but let me ask you—why would Canadian Muslims on average be any different than those in Britain? And I assure you, anyone who doesn't believe there are Canadians who support terrorism certainly hasn't listened to my show!

So many calls poured into the CFRA switchboard in support of Hezbollah and terrorism in general on August 11, 2006, the day following a foiled plot to blow up as many as ten airplanes bound from Britain to the US, that one of Canada's leading terrorist experts felt compelled to call my show with a dire warning: "Our immigration and refugee program is a death wish," said David Harris, former Chief of Strategic Planning for CSIS and now Senior Fellow for National Security for the Canadian Coalition for Democracies (a multi-ethnic, multi-religion organization with the stated goal of "defending and advancing democracy and civil liberties in a safe Canada and stable world"). "Our immigration entry system is out of control," he charged. "We cannot possibly properly screen more than a quarter million new Canadians every year, plus another 25,000 to 30,000 refugees. Furthermore, we cannot properly integrate them into Canadian society.

"Another problem that seems to be ignored," he told my audience, "is that while most people who come here from other lands want nothing more than to settle into a peaceful life, we allow radicals to infiltrate the ethnic communities. Radicals who intimidate recent arrivals into giving money for terrorist causes, often threatening family members who remain behind.

"Those who believe our open-arms policy towards immigrants will save us from terrorist attacks are naïve," he claimed. "Terrorists have already used Canada as a staging ground for attacks elsewhere, a great deal of money is being recruited here for terrorist causes, and let us never forget we have already been targeted. It is a very dangerous situation. I repeat, our immigration system is a death wish!"

Endorsing much of what Mr. Harris said was a woman who called shortly after. "I gave my name as Mary," she said. "But that's not my real name. Lowell, I've been in Canada 45 years, I have Canadian children and grandchildren, but I can tell you that even today I am afraid of some of the people in my ethnic community. In particular, some of the people who have come here recently. So afraid, that I cannot give you my real name for fear of some kind of reprisal. It's terrible what we are doing to this country!"

As for the business of loyalty, I suspect it's not just a disturbing number of Muslims who feel no sense of attachment to Canada. I mean, after all, our government believes we have a national culture that is no more worth preserving than that of the Cargo Cult of Melanesia...

THIRTY-TWO

The View From Down Under

We should have been paying much closer attention to Australian Prime Minister John Howard during his Australian Day address in January 2006. Oh, he paid tribute to his country's ethnic diversity, all right. He described it as one of "the enduring strengths of our nation." Which is about where a Canadian politician, even Stephen Harper, I am afraid, would probably stop. But Howard went on to say what we are afraid to say in this country. Listen to this from the lips of the Australian Prime Minister: "Even diverse countries have a dominant cultural pattern running through them. In Australia's case, that dominant pattern comprises Judeo-Christian ethics, the progressive spirit of the enlightenment, and the institutions and values of British political culture."

Wow! Can you imagine any Canadian politician with the guts to say anything approaching that?

Then he went on to say that his countrymen have "drawn back from being too obsessed with diversity." And listen to this from Mr. Howard:

> It would be a crushing mistake to downplay the hopes and the expectations of our national family. We expect all who come here to make an overriding commitment to

Australia, its laws and its democratic values. We expect them to master the common language of English and we will help them to do so.

We want them to learn about our history and heritage. And we expect each unique individual who joins our national journey to enrich it with their loyalty and their patriotism.

In addition, he has made it plain that newcomers to Australia owe a debt to that country, not the other way around. He wants to see all students saluting the Australian flag at morning assembly, and Australia's Education Minister has promised to end what she says is political correctness in the country's schools and to undo the damage done to the study of history by educators who "filter it through Marxist, feminist interpretations."

It's enough to make a true conservative weep with joy, at least if you live in Australia!

THIRTY-THREE

The View From Britain

Melanie Phillips, author of the best-selling book *Londonistan*, columnist with the *Daily Mail* and winner of the 1996 Orwell Prize for Journalism (see www.melaniephillips.com), wrote the following about Britain in the June 16, 2006, issue of the *National Post*, in an article entitled "The Country That Hates Itself":

Multiculturalism has exacerbated the alienation that has left so many British Muslims vulnerable to the siren song of jihad. In addition, Britain has been unravelling its identity for decades, and multiculturalism has been the outcome. Since World War II, Britain's elite has suffered from a collective collapse of cultural nerve. Many things contributed: postwar exhaustion, the collapse of the British Empire and post-colonial flagellatory guilt of the kind that white Western liberals have made their specialty.

This left the British establishment vulnerable to the revolutionary ideology of the New Left, at the core of which lay a hatred of Western society. As a consequence, the British elite decided not only that the British nation was an embarrassment, but also that the very idea of the nation was an anachronism. Britain had to be unravelled and a new world order constructed from principles unattained by the particulars of national culture.

So schools no longer transmitted the British national story and the country's bedrock values. Immigrant children were taught instead that their culture was the

I ask you, aside from the bit about losing the empire, could not those exact words be written about Canada? Have we not done exactly the same thing? Are we still not doing it?

Why? Why are we busily creating a nation that even those of my daughters' ages can scarcely recognize? A nation devoid of national culture. And to whose benefit? The latest figures indicate that immigrants today are not doing as well financially as those of a generation ago. Many newcomers report sensing a growing feeling of hostility towards them from many Canadians and, in particular, Canadians who immigrated here in the post-war years at a time when you either integrated into mainstream Canada or were sent home.

I cannot tell you the number of relatively new Canadians who have complained bitterly to me that while immigrants today get far more benefits than they ever dreamed of, those arriving these days seem far less willing to adapt and work hard the way they and their parents had to.

Ms. Phillips blames Britain's loss of national identity on what she calls "the revolutionary ideology of the New Left that has at its core a hatred of Western society." If you examine what is happening in Canada and listen very carefully, you will hear and see exactly the same ideology and not just as it applies to multiculturalism. Our reluctance to teach our children Canadian history, the gradual erosion of many of our traditions, such as Christmas, in our public schools and institutions, the terrible neglect of our military and our proud military traditions are only some of the more public manifestations of our disappearing national identity.

It's hard to believe that what is behind this is anti-Western sentiment, but it is fascinating, isn't it, that a growing number of scientists claim it is this deep-seated hatred of Western culture and capitalism that is really behind Kyoto?

Frankly, the more I look around the more convinced I become that I prefer the old Canada that was not only brave, really brave, but damn proud of it too! Imagine that! Proud of a country hewn from a cold and hostile land through unimaginable sacrifice and bravery by our ancestors from around the world. Proud of being perched at the northern end of the underground railway, the promised land for thousands of fleeing slaves. Even when my children were growing up, we all knew that this was the country that captured Vimy Ridge, that it was we who stood fast against the deadly mustard gas at the Somme; ours was the country that helped to liberate Italy, whose brave soldiers advanced further against the enemy on D-Day than those of either Britain or the US. We knew that it was Canadians who liberated Holland and were—and still are—loved for it. We knew we had the world's best hockey players, that Alexander Graham Bell invented the telephone here and made the first long-distance call between Brantford and Paris, Ontario We were proud of the fact that it was in Canada that Jackie Robinson prepared himself to break the colour barrier in the big leagues.

We even took pride in knowing we had beaten the Americans in the War of 1812. We knew all of that and a great deal more. We thought we had a wonderful heritage and culture and it wasn't until Pierre Trudeau and his camp followers informed us otherwise that we realized how mistaken we had been.

And so the "self-chosen ones" inform us smugly, in order to create this brave new Canada we must first tear down that which we had before and rebuild something far better.

The tearing down seems to be coming along quite nicely. It's the rebuilding part that worries me!

THIRTY-FOUR

The Homeless Industry

I can't stand it anymore! Traffic is light this early in the morning, so taking a chance some half-asleep idiot won't plow into me, I pull up tight to the curb, put my little Cavalier in park, punch on the four-way flashers and gingerly make my way up the sloping concrete embankment.

You can just barely see their eyes. Like those of a friendly ferret I once owned, bright, mildly curious, peeking up, or in this case down at you from a hidey-hole.

The man looks just exactly as you would expect someone to look who has lived for the better part of a year under a bridge. Red-tipped nose dripping into a dirty grey-brown beard. A rat's nest of shoulder-length hair. The rest of him rolled cocoon-like in what appears to be a mangle of blankets and old carpets. He could be anywhere from 35 to 60 years of age. Who could tell?

The woman, on the other hand, looks as though she still cares. Red-rimmed eyes, surprisingly blue in the bitter cold, a slightly shopworn but clean face, and some kind of semi-stylish cropped hair. She's almost pretty, although so encased in some kind of monster sleeping bag that there is no way of determining what secrets lie beneath!

"Listen," I say, "it's got to be nearly 10 below right now, you guys must be freezing. Would you let me find you a decent place to live?" They stare at me. I begin to wish I had minded my own business but blunder on. "I'm sure I can find you a place to live. I know you probably don't want to go to a shelter or anything like that; I'm talking about an apartment, someplace where you can have a nice warm spot and privacy as well."

The woman finally speaks. "We like it here. Why can't we stay here?" Her voice is almost childlike, whiney. The man grunts something.

I dive in even deeper. "Look, this is driving me crazy. I come to work this way every morning and for almost a year now I've seen you two living here under this bridge. It wasn't so bad in the summer but, come on, we're in the middle of winter, you're going to freeze out here."

"F—k off," says the man. "We like it here. We're warm."

He's not threatening in any way, but by this time I'm beginning to feel very uncomfortable indeed. Like an interfering idiot, if the truth were known!

They seem healthy enough. They seem warm enough, although how they can sleep at 20 or 30 below zero on a bed of sloping concrete remains a mystery to me to this day.

"Alright," I say. "Listen, can I get you anything? How about some hot coffee? Can I bring you back some coffee?"

"Don't drink coffee. Not good for you," he says. "How about you bring us some sugar?" He looks at me expectantly.

And so the next morning beneath the Bronson Avenue Bridge on Ottawa's Walkley Road, I deliver a one-pound bag of

Redpath sugar to the two who seem to have forgotten what they asked for but nonetheless appear reasonably grateful.

They remain there all winter. I read somewhere that nearby restaurants are upset because the couple keeps raiding tables for sugar. At one point I believe someone does manage to get them into a home of some kind, but they skip out one night and are back under the Bronson Avenue Bridge the next day. Home is home, after all!

One morning the following summer they are gone. I never see them again. I never even learn their names. I ask around, but no one seems to know what happened to them. Sugar is probably disappearing from restaurant tables in another town with a homey underpass. Is their story tragic? Some believe so. I'm not so sure.

While no doubt more than a bit odd, it was obvious that, unlike some with genuine mental illness, both of them knew exactly what they were doing and were living as they did out of pure choice. Modern-day hermits really, squatters under a bridge instead of in a ramshackle hut in the woods.

Perhaps as happy as any nine-to-fiver.

Perhaps as happy as you or I, living their lives unfettered by convention, clocks, or expectations. Happy with a bag of sugar. Not my choice. But theirs!

Can you say that about all our homeless?

Of course not.

Some of these homeless people have serious mental illnesses which sadly go untreated because of a left-wing ideology that believes that insisting they be hospitalized or take medication contravenes their right to wander the streets in a fog of confusion and paranoia.

A few are befuddled drug or alcohol addicts who, just as with the mentally ill, we refuse to order off the streets into treatment.

Many of our homeless, especially in the warmer months, are nothing more than young people off on a parentless summer camp-out of booze, drugs, and sex. Tom Sidney of Ottawa's Operation Go Home tells me the numbers of the so-called homeless swell by 30 to 40 percent every summer. The social activists encourage this, of course, since it helps greatly to inflate the numbers.

That's the real reason these young punks are allowed to live on the streets. They may drive local merchants crazy, cost us millions in lost tourist dollars, stab each other, and urinate on outdoor public property, but they really help to bump up the figures when the cry goes up for more money for the homeless.

Getting a firm grasp on just how much money is one of the more difficult tasks I've latched onto in recent years. Almost as tough as trying to find out where some of that ad-scam money went!

The first problem is determining just exactly how many legitimately homeless people we have in Ottawa.

The best we can do is take Statistics Canada figures on census day 2001 that indicated the capital had 1,040 homeless people. Many skeptics say this figure is vastly inflated and that, furthermore, many of those listed as homeless on that particular day are really just moving from one place to another. On the other hand, many of those in the huge homeless industry (those who earn their living from studying and occasionally actually helping the homeless) claim the figure is low.

Over the years, tens of millions of dollars have been spent on studies, surveys, conventions, and discussions, just to determine an acceptable method of counting the homeless. Please note, not tens of millions of dollars on the homeless—that figure is in the billions—but tens of millions just discussing how to count them. It's really quite astonishing.

For example, back in 1995, a three-day workshop was held at the University of Toronto to discuss how to carry out a proper head count of those without homes. Let me quote directly from a review of the workshop, written by T. Peressini, PhD, L. McDonald, PhD and D. Hulchanski PhD:

> The Workshop on Homelessness brought together a panel of experts from the United States and Canada to critically review the various definitions and methods that are currently available, and to offer recommendations concerning those that are preferred or optimal. The panel consisted of experts from government, the service community, the research community and academia.
>
> On the first day of the workshop the issue of the types of definition of homelessness that should be used was discussed and debated. Participants emerged from this debate agreeing that researchers prefer definitions that are focused on the literally homeless. These types of definition are chosen because they are relatively easy to operationalize and implement and they provide the highest return in terms of cost effectiveness and representation of the population.

Please remember. These highly paid individuals were only supposed to figure out how to count a few people. The first day was apparently spent feverishly struggling over how to define "homeless!" The next two days, believe me, were no better.

The conclusions they reached were that more funding was required and a committee was formed to further study the problem of counting the homeless. Surprise, surprise!

Dozens if not hundreds of similar studies, surveys and workshops were held in subsequent years with still no agreement on who is actually a homeless person or how to count them. This exercise continues to this day.

Forget for a moment all the agonizing over how to count the homeless; how about all the studies, workshops, and surveys that have been carried out on how to deal with whatever number of homeless there may be?

Just for the fun of it, I googled "Homeless Studies, Ontario" and came up with 72 different postings on one website alone! You can be certain that each one of those studies—and there are hundreds more—cost us thousands if not tens of thousands of dollars!

The homeless industry is huge in this country, sucking hundreds of millions of dollars away from people who are in real need of help. Among those denied real help, by the way, are those who are legitimately homeless, since very little of the money we pour into the industry ever trickles down to the people on the street.

Finding out exactly how much money is drained away into the bottomless pit of the homeless industry is almost as difficult as determining how many legitimately homeless people we have.

One of the reasons getting an accurate handle on the money is difficult is because of the plethora of agencies and organizations involved in providing services of one kind or another to the homeless. According to Lisa Stephens Immen, the former chairman of the Neighbourhood's Forum, a council of residential associations in Toronto's downtown core, there are "hundreds" of such agencies in that city, very often providing identical services and fiercely competing with each other for "clients."

As best I can determine, there are 32 such agencies in Ottawa, including private ones such as the Salvation Army, which, by the way, is one of the few organizations that eschews studies, gets down into the trenches and actually helps the homeless.

Using all the figures I can get my hands on, it would appear that the City of Ottawa pours somewhere between $30 and $35 million in total into the capital's homeless industry. That does not include private donations that, from what I understand, are considerable.

If my figures are reasonably accurate, it means that each of the some one thousand homeless people in Ottawa cost the taxpayers between $30,000 and $35,000 yearly. Yes, that is $30,000 to $35,000 per homeless person per year! That means my "sugar-loving couple" under the Bronson Avenue Bridge was costing Ottawa taxpayers about $60,000 a year. Enough to settle them into a lovely apartment and feed them like royalty.

Helping to authenticate my figures are revelations which came to light in Toronto this past spring.

On April 19, 2006, some 1,100 eager social activists fanned out across Toronto to conduct the city's first-ever census of the homeless. Some estimates had placed the homeless figure as high as 50,000. Thus you can imagine the screams of protest when the astonishing discovery was made that there were only 5,052 homeless people in a city of more than five million. So there can be no confusion, we're talking one tenth of one percent of the total population of greater Toronto.

Since Toronto last year gave $160 million to various agencies to "fix" the homeless problem, it means that the going rate per client in the Big Smoke is $31,000, about the same as my estimate of what we spend in Ottawa.

The homeless advocates claim the so-called hidden homeless weren't counted, that they must have missed hundreds if not thousands of individuals. Their fear, no doubt, is that when Toronto taxpayers get wind of the fact that each homeless person is costing them more than $30,000, demands will grow to get them all into apartments, or even on round-the-world cruises, all of which would cost far less that what we are spending now. In other words, the homeless industry might be pressured to actually get some of the homeless off the streets instead of pouring the money into conventions, workshops, studies, reports, and heaven only knows what else.

And as for failing to count properly, John Geiger, editorials editor of the *National Post,* remarked in a June 30, 2006, column entitled "What Homelessness Crisis?":

> In fact, far from underestimating homelessness, there was a real danger that the survey methods would inflate the number. By choosing one night—April 19—to undertake the homeless survey, and then publicizing that date, the city effectively encouraged every activist and like-minded hand-wringer to strategically join the ranks of the "homeless" for a couple of hours. In addition, with some 1,100 enumerators scouring the streets and literally beating the bushes in the city ravines for the homeless and because the homeless are also ambulatory, there was a higher probability of double counting than actually missing a homeless person.

By the way, as Councillor Densil Minnan-Wong points out, Toronto spends more money on the approximately five thousand homeless (.001 percent of the population) than on parks and recreation, transportation services or public health services for the 99.9 percent of the population (approximately 5 million) who are not homeless!

You've got to be way out there on the far, loony Left not to realize something is seriously out of whack with this picture but, believe it or not, the first reaction from some of Toronto's city councillors was that all that was needed to fix the problem was more money!

In his column, Geiger goes on to note that there are 4,500 shelter beds in Toronto and on April 19 only 3,649 of those beds were occupied. The survey found that only 818 were actually living on the streets and there were sufficient shelter beds to accommodate them all. A few others were in jail or being treated in hospitals.

One of the things I find fascinating with the Toronto census is that almost one quarter of all the so-called homeless are Aboriginal. As you know, we spend billions of dollars in Canada providing homes and other free services on Native reserves, so in fact about one quarter of those listed as homeless in Toronto would actually have a home available to them if they chose to live on a reserve.

Lisa Stephens Immen tells me that when she served for three years on Toronto's Homelessness Advisory Committee, her group conducted a study of rooming houses and homelessness that estimated the actual number of persons on the street (in 1997) was 3,600—far from the 50,000 plus claimed by the advocates for the homeless. When she presented these figures, which had been carefully documented, she was insulted and booed by the advocates, many of whom worked in "the industry."

Furthermore, she says, when churches and community groups began to offer "Out of the Cold" programs, which provided supper and a warm bed for the night, they were privately derided as do-gooders for not using the union-waged "professionals" employed by the social agencies.

Immen goes on to say that the "nasty little secret about the homeless advocates is that their funding depends entirely on the number of 'clients' an agency serves. So," she claims, "it is very much in their best interests to keep the figures as high as possible." She tells me that advocates often double or triple count. She pointed to the 1996 Clarke report indicating that, on average, each homeless person uses as many as 17 different agencies a month and every visit is classed as a separate homeless person. When I asked her specifically if she believed, or had evidence, that in fact one homeless person using 17 different agencies was counted as 17 homeless people, her response was succinct: "Yes."

She says the homeless advocates' refusal to countenance a survey or tracking method for those on the streets is all centered on money—they need to keep the numbers of homeless as high as possible.

"Make no mistake," Immen says, "an anonymous, unaccountable, emergency homeless person is worth big bucks to somebody. An individual with a human face, a case history, and a life to be accounted for is not."

This issue of actually tracking the homeless to find out where they are from, how many there are, why they are on the street, whether they are really homeless or just out on a lark is very interesting.

More than ten years ago, Human Resources and Development Canada (HRDC) established something called a National Homeless Shelter Tracking System, or at least an attempt was made to do so. The idea was to plug all homeless shelters into some kind of central computerized database that, among other things, would be able to track those who were using more than one agency, who had undergone addiction treatment, and so on.

Seven years later, on January 6, 2003, Juliet O'Neill, writing in the *Ottawa Citizen*, reported that, "after seven years, and more than $1.3 million spent on consulting, designing, programming, testing, updating and testing again, a national homeless information tracking system still isn't off the ground across the country."

Almost another four years has rolled by and I have news that I am sure will not shock you: Now, after ten years of endless planning, studying, writing and rewriting computer programs, consultations, and many millions more dollars wasted, the National Homeless Shelter Tracking System has disappeared into the dust, just like other grandiose programs dreamed up over the years to "resolve the homeless problem." How many millions went into this tracking system, not even HRDC can say.

Some shelters today use an internal rudimentary tracking system for their own purposes and to assist with billing various levels of governments for services provided, but there is no national tracking system and, indeed, no means of sharing information from agency to agency within a city, let alone the country. In other words, if someone is using 17 different agencies in Toronto or any city every month, there is no way of accurately tracking this, or from what I can determine, any desire to do so.

In an interview for this book, Perry Rowe, executive director of The Salvation Army, Ottawa Booth Centre, told me, "Any executive director of any shelter would tell you that if we had been able to spend all those dollars that poured into the tracking system and use them in a more creative manner, we could all have done far more to really help the homeless."

But in, fact, the millions we poured into a failed national

tracking system is peanuts compared to the mighty rivers of cash that have come flooding in from the poor beleaguered taxpayers (you and me).

How about this? In December of 1999, the Government of Canada, once again through HRDC, announced it was "investing" $753 million over three years under something called the National Homeless Initiative (NHI) to help alleviate or prevent homelessness.

Where did all this money disappear?

Excellent question. Not that I can provide the answer. I tried for the better part of five months to track down this money. No luck. Some of it probably did end up in the coffers of various municipalities, and may actually have been used to help alleviate or prevent homelessness, but from what I can determine, once again the bulk of the money was flushed down the monster maw of research, planning, analyzing, conventions, workshops, evaluating, analyzing the evaluation...ah hell, you get the picture!

If you don't believe that most of this money was flushed down the toilet of Alice in Wonderland bureaucracy, let me quote just one paragraph of a 96-page government report entitled "Evaluation Approach":

> Case Study approach: The evaluation methodology is based primarily on a set of 20 community case studies that characterize the implementation, early outcomes and immediate incremental impact of the Support Communities Partnership Initiative (SCPI). Aboriginal homelessness and youth homelessness components of the NHI. Case studies involved a review of documents (community plans, project reports, etc.) as well as key informant interviews with HRDC staff, community organizations, non-governmental service delivery staff, project clients and officials from other levels of government.
>
> In addition, information on all 61 SCPI communities was collected through the analysis of program data and documents and interviews with stakeholders."

And no, I swear I did not make any of that up—check it out at http://www11.hrdc-drhc.gc.ca/pls/edd/SPAH203_03_343003.htm.

Aside from those stakeholder interviews, it sure doesn't sound like the homeless were involved in all of this at all. And as a matter of fact, I am not even sure if the reference to stakeholder actually means an interview with a homeless person! Ninety-six pages of pure bureaucratic whale poop piled on top of overripe buffalo chips—all of it pouring millions if not tens of millions of dollars into the pockets of armies of social activists, pollsters, researchers, professors, psychiatrists, psychologists, computer programmers, analysts…ah hell, again you get the picture. If any of this actually helped a single homeless person find a place to live it was probably purely by accident.

But let's pursue this business of taxpayers' money being dumped into a bottomless pit for about one tenth of one percent of our big city population.

The $753 million dumped in by the federal government was topped up by an additional $553 million from the provinces and municipalities.

Then, in 2002, the federal government said, ah, what the heck, we can't waste all of our money on Quebec advertising firms and the gun registry—what say we kick in another $403 million for the homeless industry? And so they did.

Don't think for a moment that's the end of it.

In addition to all of the "Let's get rid of the homeless programs" is the, "Let's build lots and lots of cheap housing for the homeless programs." So in 2001, the federal government coughed up $680 million to build 40,000 new housing units over five years. That amount was matched by the provinces, so add another $680 million of our money!

Have the 40,000 units actually been built? No, no—don't laugh. You must understand, before you can build government housing, you've got to do research, stakeholders must be interviewed, and on, and on, and on... And not a piece of lumber or power tool in sight yet!

Apparently about 2,200 low-cost homes have actually been built with all that money, or might be built, or are planned to be built sometime, someplace, maybe. Is the $1.36 billion still there? Who knows? Weeks of research and interviews have left me and you totally in the dark!

They've ripped millions more from our pockets in the past two or three years to fix the "homeless problem." It's all so convoluted and the money pours in from so many sources that I doubt if even Sheila Fraser could track it all down. As a matter of fact that's a heck of a good idea! I suspect if we ever did learn where all the money has gone that we've poured into the "homeless problem" in the past decade we'd have enough to build every Canadian a nice little cabin in the woods someplace where we could escape, at least for a few days from the madness that is overtaking this country.

The tactics used to suck all this money out of us without in any way helping actual homeless people is taken right from the left-wing recipe book! Remember how it's done?

First create the appearance of a crisis.

Well, I ask you, what could be a greater crisis than a NATIONAL DISASTER?!

• • •

It all started in Toronto. On October 28, 1998, Toronto City Council, one of the most left-wing in all of North America, declared that: HOMELESSNESS IS A NATIONAL DISASTER IN CANADA! As you can imagine, the media went wild with this, running stories quoting "experts" and social activists claiming among other things that as many as a quarter million Canadians, including thousands of seniors and pregnant women, were sleeping on the streets.

The following day, Councillors Wendy Byrne and Alex Munter presented a motion to the Community Services Committee of Ottawa Regional Council declaring—you guessed it—HOMELESSNESS IS A NATIONAL DISASTER IN CANADA!

I've tried to track down all the other cities, organizations, churches, unions, and so on, that have, over the years, declared HOMELESSNESS IS A NATIONAL DISASTER IN CANADA! I lost count at 27. The screaming has been wonderfully effective. Almost immediately after another newspaper discovers that HOMELESSNESS IS A NATIONAL DISASTER IN CANADA, one level of government or another pumps a few million more into the "national disaster pot!"

If you just add up the figures from the federal and provincial governments in the past eight years, it totals almost $4 billion. That doesn't include the money poured in by various municipalities or private and church groups. In Ottawa, for example, it costs about $45 to put a homeless person up for the night in a shelter. The City of Ottawa contributes only $35 per night, which means that in the case of the Salvation Army, they must kick in about $10 per night from donations collected during the year. Different shelters in different cities across

Canada have different arrangements, but there is no question that in addition to the billions in taxes, millions more in private donations are spent each year on the homeless.

And please keep this in mind: Since many cities and towns in Canada have no homeless people, or only a tiny handful, we are probably talking here about far less than one tenth of one percent of the country's population!

So the next time a panhandler hits you up for some spare change, ask yourself this question: Did he get any of these billions of dollars we are spending to find him a place to live? Did the guy who's sprawled across a grate on Yonge Street in Toronto get any of this money? What about my "sugar couple" under the Bronson Avenue Bridge? It would appear not.

So I ask you, then, where did the money go?

To find out, I guess we'll need to conduct studies, research, workshops, polls, evaluations, conferences, discussion papers, fill out reports, and analyze the studies. We'll have to call in experts, social scientists, professors, psychiatrists, psychologists, vegetarians, veterinarians, massage therapists, wart removers…ah hell, you get the picture!

THIRTY-FIVE

Voices

I'm watching, fascinated, as Daniel's [not his real name] skilled hands work the wood. Sure, confident, and quick. The hands of an artist. Hands that can make beautiful music with a power saw or an electric guitar.

I'm unsure exactly what he's making, but from a jumble of two-by-twos gradually appears a uniquely designed backyard childproof gate. He hasn't seen me pull into the driveway, so I swing the car door open. "Hey, Danny boy, don't believe what everybody else says, you're doing a hell of a job!" It's an old joke with us. "Ya," says Daniel, "I just wish I could say the same about you. Did you put in your three hours again today?" He chuckles and goes back to work.

Daniel, like most craftsmen these days, is in great demand and doesn't come cheap, believe me, but if you want the job done right, there's none better. I just wish I could afford him!

The voices don't bother him anymore. They're much quieter now, less frequent. He's learned to deal with them, just as he's learned to deal with so much more in his young life.

We're all very proud of him.

Eleven years ago, on his eighteenth birthday, this very bright, handsome, gifted musician began to hear voices urging him to do strange things. Frightened, his mother rushed him first to the Royal Ottawa Hospital, then to the Queensway Carleton Hospital where he was diagnosed with schizophrenia, a serious brain disorder that, according to the Schizophrenia Society of Canada, is believed to be caused by a biochemical imbalance. The symptoms include auditory and/or visual hallucinations, extreme paranoia, and fear. It strikes one in every 100 Canadians.

And thus began a life-and-death struggle against the disease and, almost as difficult, against a cruel and dangerous ideology that seemed determined to keep him from receiving the treatment he needed, not only to cure his symptoms, but to literally keep him alive!

The attempts to prevent his recovery began almost immediately.

Two days after Daniel's admission to hospital, he began to show the first signs of recovery. The drugs were doing their job. While the voices hadn't stopped, he was gradually becoming more rational, his speech had returned to nearly normal. He no longer asked that someone "knarl him a longbird" when he wanted a cigarette. His parents began to hope that with continued proper treatment, including a combination of some of the new "miracle drugs," time, and patience, Daniel could return to a productive, useful life.

Doctors warn that full recovery from schizophrenia is usually a very slow process with one of the greatest problems being the fact that many patients, after release from hospital, fail to take their medication and, as a result, are likely to relapse.

Daniel's parents, as you might expect, were determined this would not happen and resolved to ensure that their son would comply with every medical protocol. "If the proper medication can restore Daniel to his normal self," they told his doctor, "you can be certain we'll make sure he follows all instructions."

Little did they know.

On the third day of his hospitalization Daniel's father received a strange phone call from his son. The young man's voice was cold, distant, and uncharacteristically angry: "My lawyer tells me I don't have to stay here and I don't have to take any drugs either." Before the flabbergasted father could respond, Daniel concluded, "and he showed me the legal document that says you can't stop me from leaving here either."

His parents rush to the hospital, but it's too late. Despite attempts by his doctor and several nurses, Daniel has walked out of the hospital, without a cent to his name, without his medication. In a state of extreme paranoia, he believes his parents, doctors and nurses are trying to imprison him and fill him with dangerous drugs.

According to the government of the day, this is all in Daniel's best interests! Thanks to the Patient Advocacy Act, as part of the Mental Health Act of Ontario passed by Premier Bob Rae in 1992, there was nothing anyone, including Daniel's parents, could legally do to stop him from leaving the hospital or to compel him to take medication.

The man Daniel believed was his lawyer was actually a poorly trained, non-professional "Ontario Advocacy Commission Rights Advisor" who was empowered to read every newly arrived mentally ill patient their legal rights under changes made to the Ontario Mental Health Act by the NDP government of Bob Rae. Even those suffering from serious mental illness were given the full "rights" treatment, which included advice that under the law they could leave hospital at any time and were not compelled to take whatever medication was prescribed.

On the same day the "advisor" insisted on telling Daniel that he could leave the hospital any time and didn't have to take his medication, he visited another patient in a nearby bed and told him the same thing.

That young man, only two days previously, had to be restrained in the nearby recreation room after throwing billiard balls at the walls. Even while heavily sedated in his bed, the "rights advisor" informed this poor man that he too could get up and leave at any time.

Whether that patient actually left at the time is unclear; there was a provision in the Act that allowed doctors to restrain a patient if they could prove he posed an "imminent" danger to himself or to others. We can only hope that provision was exercised.

These "advocacy commissioners" didn't just turn up at the bedsides of schizophrenia patients. If you had a relative institutionalized with Alzheimer's or dementia during those Bob Rae days, they were probably told much the same thing as Daniel.

Faced with a serious deterioration of their mother's mental health, my wife and her sister spent months working to get her admitted to the very fine Homewood Institution in Guelph. No sooner was their mother admitted than one of these "rights" advisors showed up to inform her she did not have to stay there. At the time, their mother was in such an advanced state of dementia she was totally unaware of who or where she was!

Fortunately, the poor woman very quickly forgot the advice! Can you imagine? If, in fact, their mother had left the Homewood she would have been totally lost before she even exited the front door.

It certainly gives you an idea of the almost religious fervour propelling the whole "patients' rights" movement in Ontario at the time.

My wife's mother lived out her final days at the Homewood, but Daniel took the advice of the man he believed was his lawyer, walked out of the hospital and wasn't seen or heard from for several days until he appeared back in the emergency ward of another hospital. He was almost incoherent this time.

His very angry father phoned David Reville, the Bob Rae appointed Chair of the Ontario Advocacy Commission. When Daniel's father related what had happened and pointed out the manner in which it had seriously set back his son's treatment and even risked his life, Mr. Reville responded angrily, "It's none of your business."

"But I'm his father. Of course it's my business," he began to say, but was cut off by a very agitated Mr. Reville, who repeated that since Daniel was over the age of 14 he could make his own decisions concerning health care and "no one, including his father, had any right to interfere." And hung up.

By the way, I was present when that phone call was made and heard every word of it. It is not something easily forgotten, believe me! It's one of the reasons I see red to this day when people tell me they vote NDP. I cannot tell you how I feel about the possibility of Bob Rae becoming Prime Minister of this country. Because it was Bob Rae and his government who let this incredible left-wing misguided ideology persist for as long as he remained in power.

And it's not as if he wasn't warned. In September of 1992, before the Advocacy Act and the Consent to Treatment Act were passed, the Ontario College of Physicians and Surgeons stated publicly that this kind of legislation was so seriously flawed it could endanger members of the public needing medical care. Doctors, psychiatrists, and health care workers at almost every level fought it tooth and nail, but to no avail. Once again, ideology won the day. Forget what doctors, psychiatrists, and other professionals who would have to deal with the new legislation on a daily basis had to say. I mean, what the heck would they know?

During a committee hearing on February 6, 1996, as the newly elected Mike Harris Conservative Government debated whether to scrap the Act, David Reville boasted that his advisors had given "rights" advice under the Mental Health Act to more than 600 mental patients each month.

This bit of information sends chills up my spine!

Talk to anyone who has ever had a loved one hospitalized in Ontario with a severe mental illness during the NDP tenure and I'm sure you will hear similar stories. In essence, those advocacy commissioners were saying "Try and get out and don't come back" to mentally ill people. Keep in mind that some of the patients were so confused they believed they were getting messages directly from God or that they could fly!

Advising him of his rights almost cost Daniel his life. Now convinced that he didn't have to stay in hospital or take his medication, he began a dangerous dance with death. His physical health was deteriorating; in fact, he was down to almost skin and bones. At one point, convinced that aliens were about to attack him, he leapt from a second-storey window. He ended up in hospital again, this time with severely injured heels.

One of the major problems with the legislation in effect at the time was that he could not be committed to hospital without his consent unless he posed what doctors considered to be an "imminent" threat to himself or others. Simply wasting away, living on the street at 25 below or believing aliens were chasing you was simply not good enough to get you hospitalized.

To make matters worse, with so much emphasis being placed on patients' rights, rather than patients' needs, doctors were very reluctant to commit even a seriously psychotic person to hospital. Defining "imminent danger" is a virtually impossible task when dealing with totally irrational people who might sleep one day away, then jump off a bridge the next.

This is actually what happened when Daniel was first rushed to hospital, panic stricken and increasingly paranoid, with voices shouting at him from every direction. His mother's first inclination was to take him to the Royal Ottawa Hospital. Believe it or not, despite all the symptoms of severe psychosis and an obviously very disturbed patient, the Royal Ottawa turned him away. Not in any "imminent" danger they said! Come back in six weeks, was the advice.

Fortunately, the Queensway Carleton Hospital, which was their next stop, admitted him immediately.

His parents and others tried desperately many times over the ensuing years to convince Daniel to remain in hospital long enough to recover sufficiently to allow himself to make rational decisions. You have no idea how difficult it is to convince an irrational person to make a rational life-and-death decision, especially when both the Ontario Government and the Canadian Mental Health Association come down on the side of the irrational patient!

Daniel's father had almost succeeded in convincing his son that the Ontario Government could be dismissed as complete idiots who wished to do him harm, when along came the Canadian Mental Health Association (CMHA) stating publicly that they too didn't believe a mentally ill person should be compelled to take medication.

Daniel, even in a delusional state, is extremely bright, reads the newspapers, listens to radio and pays special attention to anything concerning mental illness. It was only natural, then, that he learned of the CMHA's statement and took it as evidence that his parents were trying to imprison him, or worse. Extreme paranoia and fear, after all, are key symptoms of schizophrenia. Once again he fled the hospital in the middle of treatment and there was nothing anyone could do to stop him!

At this point Daniel's father was so desperate and so angry he phoned the Ottawa office of the CMHA and told them he was going to drop his son off at their office so they could deal with him. He didn't do it, of course, but to this day claims he wishes he had.

Daniel's story is fairly typical of what happened and to a lesser degree is still happening across this country.

Left-wing ideology is so all-consuming, so powerful that any semblance of common sense is abandoned and thousands of innocent lives are placed at risk.

What saved Daniel's life was Brian's Law, passed by the Ontario Government on December 1, 2000.

For the first time, Daniel's parents and his doctors had some authority to hold him in hospital and provide the kind of treatment which very clearly not only saved his life, but restored him to the bright, happy, highly productive person he is today.

Brian's Law is named for Brian Smith, who before his death was a very popular sportscaster and athlete in Ottawa, a former member of the NHL Los Angeles Kings.

He was shot and killed in 1995 by a man who was suffering from schizophrenia but had refused treatment, despite the advice of his psychiatrists. Thanks to Ontario's Advocacy Act, just as with Daniel, he had a legal right to refuse the treatment.

Largely due to the efforts of Brian's wife Alana Kainz, the Mike Harris Government was persuaded to make major changes to the Mental Health Act, thus giving mental health authorities more power to hold and treat a person who is severely mentally ill. And very importantly, the ability to intervene at an earlier stage in the illness.

Prior to passage of Brian's Law, officials could only intervene when a person was an "imminent" risk to himself or others. Declining health or lifestyle could not be considered. Thus a person could slowly starve to death, jump from second-storey windows, or wander the streets screaming at the top of their lungs and there was nothing legally that could be done.

With Brian's Law, the word "imminent" was removed from the act and today, with the new legislation, a patient's deteriorating mental or physical condition can be taken into account. No longer do we have to sit around and do nothing while someone we care about slowly slips to near death before being eligible for treatment.

Another major improvement is that today, with Brian's Law, physicians may recommend treatment in the community even without the patient's consent if it is determined the patient is incapable of making a rational decision and a substitute decision maker authorizes it. This substitute decision maker can be a health professional, a parent or a spouse, or someone else approved by the courts.

These community treatment orders (CTOs) apply only to people who meet specific criteria. They must have been hospitalized previously a number of times and be able to follow a treatment program.

After years of revolving-door hospital care and having demonstrated that medication, when taken, was very effective, Daniel met all the criteria; his parents obtained a court order and were able to get him hospitalized for eight weeks. Thankfully, it was long enough for the medication to do its work. Eight weeks later, he emerged from hospital determined to continue taking his medication and make a new life for himself.

The nightmare had lasted for seven years!

Now, four years after walking out of that hospital for the last time, he is a new man and everyone who knows him and his struggle is overjoyed and very proud of him.

When I told Daniel I was writing about him in this book, he asked me to say the following: "When I was psychotic, I didn't think I should have to take my medication. Now that I am not psychotic, I firmly believe I and everyone who can benefit should!"

In other words, in his opinion, you have to be psychotic in order not to believe that a psychotic person shouldn't have to take the medication that will still the voices, replace hallucinations with reality, and allow trust, love, and happiness to blossom once again.

Sadly, other stories are not always as happy.

Even with the new Brain's Law, there are some serious flaws. One of them is that without the patient's consent, he or she can only be kept in hospital for 72 hours unless a "substitute decision maker can be found to decide otherwise." Once again, this is thanks to the lobbying efforts of the "self-chosen ones" who even today continue to claim that forced treatment violates a person's rights, even if it saves their life.

Other safeguards have been introduced so that smart lawyers and other advocates can still win at insisting that it is in the best interests of their clients to keep wandering the streets without treatment.

A 1997 Clarke Institute of Psychiatry report found that fully 60 percent of the so-called street people have diagnosable mental illnesses. Which tells you just about everything you need to know about this modern-day tragedy of mentally ill people living on the streets—the very same people who berate us for the homeless problem turn around and insist that we should not have the right to help them!

It seems obvious to me that if the "homeless industry" really wished to get people off the streets and into better living conditions they would utilize the "substitute decision maker" clause in Brian's Law. Instead of holding discussions, round tables and surveys, they should establish a cadre of qualified, properly trained "substitute decision makers," utilize Brian's Law, and get those with serious mental illnesses off the streets and into treatment. In fact, when you think about it, you have to wonder why it wasn't the "homeless industry" that lobbied for the changes in Ontario's Mental Health Act created by Brian's Law. If some 60 percent of your "clients" have serious mental illness, you'd think getting them treatment would be your first priority!

THIRTY-SIX

The Last Word

Al Chandler was a little gnome of a man. Almost as broad as he was high. Fingers so thick typewriters balked. Two keys smashed at a time when only one was intended. The running joke around the radio station when he hired me was that he dared not even pause at a street corner for fear a dog mistook him for a fire hydrant!

But he was one hell of a newsman. The best I ever worked for. "Graduated summa cum laude from the school of hard knocks," he boasted. Very little formal education, bright, well-read, tenacious, and crazy about accuracy. "Assumption is the bane of good journalism," he pounded into our rookie heads. He drove us crazy. We loved him!

It was in his capacity as news director for radio station CKPC in Brantford, Ontario, that Al hired me in 1956 as his "legman." Legman, as I soon learned, meant not only covering every Brantford event imaginable night and day for CKPC but being dragged by Al to every major news story within a hundred miles, usually it seemed, at about three in the morning!

I'm not sure if station owner Mrs. Buchanan, or Mrs. "B"

as we called her, was aware that while she paid Al well to run her radio news department, his first love was covering Southwestern Ontario as a correspondent for the now-defunct *Toronto Telegram.*

Nor am I sure if Al had decided I was the protegé he was going to pass his skills along to, or if he just wanted a strong back and weak mind to lug his huge Crown Graphic camera and the several tons of equipment (or so it seemed) necessary to operate the thing. I won't go into detail about news cameras in the mid 1950s but urge you to see one of those vintage films with the shouting newsmen with their giant fedoras and flash cameras the size of basketballs. If you see a really short guy with fingers the size of Italian sausages clutching one of those cameras—that's Al.

Al, God rest his soul, taught me many things, but none so important as that which prompted me to write this book.

We were in Ingersoll doing a feature for the *Telegram* on veteran NHL linesman George Hayes, who, by the way, is now in the Hockey Hall of Fame. We had more than enough information for the story; the problem was the photograph to accompany it. Al, it seemed to me, was taking an inordinate amount of time setting it up. Fretting about the light, the background. He couldn't seem to get George posed just right. I could see that our "model," who was known as a rebel and not averse to taking the odd drink, was getting a little testy. "Geeze, Al," I said, "you've got about a half dozen good shots, why don't we call it a day?"

I recall his response as if it were yesterday. He stopped, turned around to face me, and in a voice loud enough to be heard a block away, said, "Good? Good! Of course, they're good. That's not the point! It's not a question of how good you are, it's how good you could be!"

And when we finally did get that picture and it was featured on the sports front of the weekend *Telly* it was just that. As good as Al Chandler could be. And that, my friend, was mighty good!

I've got Al Chandler's motto up on my office wall:

"It's not a question of how good you are. It's how good you could be!"

Which is why I decided to write this book.

Yes, this is a good country. A very good country. But with everything we have inherited, from our natural resources to the foundations so carefully and often painfully laid down by our pioneering forebears, it's not a question of how good the country is, but rather how good it could be!

Do you ever think of that? How good the country could be? How good the country *should* be?

Or is good, good enough? For the sake of my grandchildren, I sure hope not.

How about you?

That's it for now from "The Island of Sanity"…

Lowell